THE ZODIAC REVISITED
Volume 3
Tying It All Together

THE ZODIAC REVISITED
Volume 3

Tying It All Together

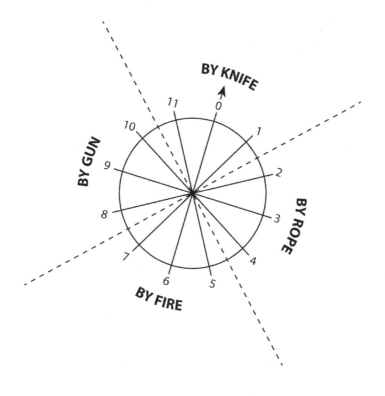

Michael F. Cole

Twin Prime Publishing
Folsom, California

ISBN 978-1-955816-02-1 (Hardcover Edition)
ISBN 978-0-9963943-2-1 (Paperback Edition)
ISBN 978-0-9963943-5-2 (ePub Edition)
ISBN 978-0-9963943-8-3 (Kindle Edition)

Library of Congress Control Number: 2020918277

Edited by Jennifer Huston
Cover design by Derek Murphy
Cover map © OpenStreetMap contributors

The column "Your Mirror Can Also See Inside You" by Count Marco in the *San Francisco Chronicle* reproduced with permission of the Newspaper Indexing Center, Micro Photo Division, B via the Copyright Clearance Center.

Excerpts from the *Vallejo Times-Herald* reproduced with permission.

Printed in the United States of America
First printing 2020

Published by Twin Prime Publishing
Folsom, California
zodiacrevisited.com

This book is dedicated to the memories of the following young men and women. Some definitely were victims of the man who called himself the Zodiac; others probably were. Regardless, all left this world much too soon and under circumstances of senseless tragedy.

- Robert Domingos
- Linda Edwards
- Johnny Ray Swindle
- Joyce Swindle
- Cheri Jo Bates
- David Faraday
- Betty Lou Jensen
- Darlene Ferrin
- Cecelia Shepard
- Paul Stine
- Richard Radetich
- Donna Lass

Although the passage of time has rendered the opportunity for justice an impossibility, it's my sincere hope that one day the world will know the name of the person or persons responsible for your unjust fates.

Contents

1

The Question of Southern California

Circumstantial evidence is not only sufficient, but may also be more certain, satisfying and persuasive than direct evidence.

US Supreme Court, *Rogers v. Missouri Pacific Railroad Co.*, 1957

One of the most nagging questions in the case of the Zodiac is whether or not the killer committed a string of murders in Southern California prior to orchestrating his reign of terror in the San Francisco Bay Area. Did he begin his foray into serial murder on a cold December night in 1968 or a warm summer day in 1963? Did his sophomore misdeed take place in a Vallejo parking lot or on a beach in San Diego? Did he first engage in post-offense communication with Bay Area newspapers or the Riverside *Press–Enterprise*?

Having developed an understanding of the Zodiac — in terms of the man, his persona, his motivations, and his methodology — and having reviewed the facts of the proposed Southern California crimes, we are now in a position to step back and consider these questions from the relevant angles. Unsurprisingly, we will not be able to arrive at answers that satisfy everyone; some — especially those who have a vested interest in believing otherwise — will find reason to take exception. But by considering all of the evidence, we will uncover answers that, I submit, have the strongest probability of being correct.

1.1   Crime Similarities

The task of substantively comparing the Southern California murders to the criminal actions of the Zodiac is a formidable one. Numerous aspects of the relevant crimes as well as their respective circumstances and investigations deserve our attention. Even deciding upon how we approach the evidence presents a challenge. Yet, in the final analysis, it's the crimes that are the most fundamental element of comparison. The crimes are at the center of the question "Was the same man responsible?" All indirect evidence, much of which is undeniably significant, derives from the crimes. For this reason, the most logical place to start our analytical journey is with the crimes themselves.

1.1.1   Motive and Victim Selection

Few would disagree that the Zodiac murders and the Southern California slayings were instances of what is known as stranger murder, in other words, homicides in which the victim was a stranger to the perpetrator. Within law enforcement communities, stranger murders are notorious for being the most difficult cases to solve because the lack of relationship between perpetrator and victim provides very little opportunity for investigators to start at the victim and work their way backward to the killer. To put it simply, the cases often provide few clues.

Of course, it's impossible to commit the act of murder without somehow choosing a victim. In the borrowed words of the Zodiac himself, " ... a victom must be found."* In the case of a stranger murder, this choice, in and of itself, provides the opportunity for investigators to gain insight into the inner workings of the killer's psyche. In fact, given that there is no other relationship between murderer and victim, understanding the killer's probable victim-selection process becomes one of the main avenues of insight. In particular, when the goal is simply to murder and other motivations such as sexual assault and monetary gain are not in play, the decision of whom to kill often represents some type of symbolic value to the person committing the act. As a murderer driven to take the life of some unknown person, the killer literally has millions of potential victims from which to choose. Why he ultimately settles on one or two victims to the exclusion of all others often involves a meaningful underlying motivation. Whether consciously or subconsciously, the killer is likely communicating some nontrivial message describing why he feels the need to lash out against society. An example of this is the case of Ted Kaczynski, also known as the Unabomber. Kaczynski targeted victims that he perceived to be contributing to society's evolving problems centered around technological progress. He didn't know the victims personally; he chose them because they symbolized the problem that was motivating him to the point of action.

This type of symbolism is unmistakable in the extended crimes of the Zodiac.* Specifically, five of these attacks involved lovestruck couples seeking romantic isolation, namely: Robert Domingos and Linda Edwards, Joyce and Johnny Ray Swindle, David Faraday and Betty Lou Jensen, Mike Mageau and Darlene Ferrin, and Bryan Hartnell and Cecelia Shepard. Furthermore, several of the remaining crimes involved lone females, as was the case with Cheri Jo Bates, Kathleen Johns, and Donna Lass.

---

*The Zodiac's *Mikado* Letter.

*As defined in *The Zodiac Revisited, Volume 2*, the "extended crimes of the Zodiac" include all the crimes that I believe the Zodiac committed including the Southern California crimes, the standard Zodiac crimes, and the murders of Richard Radetich and Donna Lass.

Taken together, the victim selection in the Southern California murders is strikingly consistent with the victim selection seen in the crimes of the Zodiac. Furthermore, the selection conveys an underlying motivation centered around a psychopathic hatred of women — especially young, desirable women — and, to a lesser extent, the men who were capable of forming meaningful, intimate relationships with them. When circumstances were amenable, the killer preferred to victimize this type of lovestruck couple, particularly in the early stages of his evolution as the Zodiac. On the other hand, when circumstances placed additional constraints on victim selection, the killer was willing to back off the need for assailing couples and settle for directing his murderous intentions toward the primary target of his hatred, namely women.

The person who came to understand these characteristics of the Southern California killer, almost immediately, was Santa Barbara County Sheriff James Webster. Though misinformation and a red-herring suspect known only as "Sandy" confused the issue, Webster nonetheless realized that the murders of Domingos and Edwards in Gaviota, California, lacked an obvious motive. Accordingly, in the fall of 1963, just months after this murder, Webster warned law enforcement agencies in other Southern California coastal areas that the killer might well resurface, with the intention of killing a similarly lovestruck couple. That warning would prove to be prescient a few months later when Joyce and Johnny Ray Swindle were inexplicably gunned down in San Diego. Sheriff Webster and other members of law enforcement suggested a single killer may have been responsible — a single killer whom they referred to as a "Sweetheart Slayer."[1]

These events are noteworthy because they provide a compelling link between Gaviota, San Diego, and the initial crimes of the Zodiac, but they also suggest an explanation of what motivated the killer to change his pattern in the murder of Cheri Jo Bates in Riverside. In the days following the San Diego murders, it's a near certainty that the killer would have read the *Los Angeles Times* in order to see what was being reported about his most recent crime, whereupon he would have found Sheriff Webster's comments. In order to minimize the probability of being caught, the man committed his second set of murders nearly 250 miles away from the first. Regardless, Sheriff Webster immediately proclaimed that the same man was quite likely responsible for both the Gaviota murders and those in San Diego and tagged him as a Sweetheart Slayer — all of which was exactly right. In response, the killer laid low for a substantially longer period of time. A short eight months separated the murders in Gaviota and San Diego. By the time Cheri Jo Bates was murdered in Riverside, more than two and a half years had passed since an unknown assailant had gunned down the Swindles. And, of course, the attack of a lone woman makes the connection to the Sweetheart Slayer considerably less obvious. If the killer's change in timing and victimology was indeed a response to Sheriff Webster's insightful observations, it seems to have worked impressively well in that no other reports of the time suggested a possible link between Cheri's murder and the previous homicides.

Furthermore, insights gleaned from The Confession clearly support the idea of a perpetrator who was motivated by a psychopathic hatred of young women, which, in fact, is consistent with the high-level motivation seen in the Gaviota and San Diego slayings.

The first of the murders that police attribute to the Zodiac took place just a little over two years after Cheri Jo Bates was killed in Riverside. By the time the killer emerged in the Bay Area, he was no longer concerned with minimizing the probability of law enforcement recognizing his crimes. To the contrary, he very much wanted law enforcement and the public to associate his crimes with his criminal persona. For this reason, and as part of an effort to establish an identity, the killer returned to his preferred victim profile — couples.

1.1.2   Gaviota and Lake Berryessa

One of the most striking similarities between the crimes of the Zodiac and the three instances of murder in Southern California is the similarity in modus operandi used in the commission of the Gaviota and Lake Berryessa attacks. In both cases, the killer, brandishing a firearm, approached a couple in a secluded spot at the water's edge. Moreover, both perpetrators came prepared with precut lengths of rope, provided the rope to their respective victims, and instructed one to tie up the other. Of course, the Gaviota perpetrator lost control of the situation and, consequently, shot his victims. At Lake Berryessa, the killer likely learned from his prior mistakes and took additional precautions. In fact, the mistakes likely provided the impetus for the killer to conceive of the need to choose an environment and a means by which he could effectively manipulate his victims — a practice I refer to as premeditated situational control.

The similarities of these two crimes is difficult to overstate. It's no surprise that when Santa Barbara County Detective William Baker sent out a statewide all-points bulletin (APB) requesting information for other crimes that were possibly related to the Gaviota murders, San Francisco Homicide Inspector William Armstrong and Special Agent Mel Nicolai from the California Department of Justice recognized the connection to the Zodiac immediately. This replication of victim selection, environment, and modus operandi — including a lack of evidence pointing toward more common motivating factors such as a desire to commit sexual assault or robbery — makes the linkage between these two crimes profoundly compelling.

1.1.3 Premeditation

Many actions in the extended crimes of the Zodiac exhibit an exceptionally high degree of premeditation. Starting with Gaviota, the scene was very accommodating in that people were unlikely to arrive at the location through any means other than driving. Therefore, the killer could interpret a single car in the small parking area just off Highway 101 as a strong indication that the car's occupants were the only people on the nearby beach. In the specific case of Domingos and Edwards, Linda had left her purse in the car such that it was visible from the outside.[2] From this, the killer could infer that at least one of the car's occupants was female. Furthermore, the path from the highway to the waterfront was a hike, which meant that the sounds of gunfire, screams, or calls for help would likely go unnoticed by anyone who happened to drive by.

The next crime in the chronology — near the beach in San Diego — showed an equally significant degree of preselection. In describing the sniper's nest location from which the killer started shooting Joyce and Johnny Ray Swindle, the San Diego Police Department (SDPD) wrote:

> *He was in total darkness and well hidden from any angle. The patio was illuminated enough to make identification of the victims by the killer a possibility and leave no doubt he knew the sex and approximate age of both victims.*[3]

These types of accommodating circumstances are not the product of a rash crime. The killer clearly invested time and effort finding this location for his sniper's nest, which perfectly concealed his position while providing him with the opportunity to target a lovestruck couple enjoying each other's company at the ocean's edge.

The killer's choice of ammunition hints at another dimension of premeditation. In Gaviota, Robert was shot eleven times, Linda was shot eight times, and the killer discharged his weapon no less than twenty-six times.[4] In order to fire that number of shots, it would have been necessary for him to reload his weapon.[5] San Diego was a different type of crime scene. One could argue it was isolated. However, it was considerably less isolated than Gaviota. Therefore, the killer would have been wise not to spend the time required to discharge so many shots. These changing constraints may well explain why the killer opted for the hollow-point ammunition.[6] With hollow-point bullets designed to inflict maximum damage, the killer could accomplish his murderous deed with fewer shots, which is precisely what he did, shooting Johnny Ray four times and Joyce three.[7] Serial killer Edmund Kemper — who murdered ten people, including six university coeds, before being apprehended in 1973 — similarly transitioned from normal .22-caliber bullets to the hollow-point variety specifically because of their increased lethality. The change was quite effective, and he was subsequently pleased with the results.[8] Likely, the Southern California killer engaged in a similar thought process, at least for this crime.

As discussed in *The Zodiac Revisited, Volume 2*, Section 2.2.1, Cheri Jo Bates's murder is the first definite instance of premeditated situational control — a very specific form of premeditation. Furthermore, the crime scene and its environment suggest that the killer likely selected the location ahead of time. The essential components of this crime required: (a) access to a lone young woman's car and (b) a nearby area in which the attack could be perpetrated, ideally providing some degree of privacy and possibly darkness. The Riverside Community College library was a nearly perfect location in terms of satisfying these constraints. Undoubtedly, lone young women frequented the library. Additionally, as a community college, a fair number of students likely drove to the destination. Finally, assuming the killer did research the location ahead of time, he would have realized that the two nearby houses — the ones between which he murdered Cheri — were abandoned and, therefore, provided the requisite privacy and darkness.[9] In fact, from the perpetrator's perspective, the only downside to the location was the presence of the nearby apartments that yielded several earwitnesses who heard Cheri's screams in what turned out to be the final moments of her life.[10] Perhaps the killer anticipated that residents would be reluctant to call the police under the circumstances; if so, he was exactly right.

The Zodiac's first two crimes in the Bay Area were blitz-style attacks on couples parked in lovers' lanes. As noted in Chapter 3 of *The Zodiac Revisited, Volume 2*, the killer was likely driven by a methodology at this point, which in and of itself represents a high degree of premeditation. The locations certainly facilitated the execution of the crimes, however, this conclusion is not surprising since lovers' lanes necessarily involve some degree of isolation. Nonetheless, the perpetrator almost certainly sought out these locations prior to the commission of the crimes based on a combination of methodology and desired crime-scene characteristics.

The call that the killer placed to the Vallejo Police Department after the Blue Rock Springs attack was yet another element of premeditation. Nancy Slover, the switchboard operator who received the call, described it by saying: "[The] subject seemed to be reading or had rehearsed what he was saying."[11] A similar argument can be made for the call following the deadly events at Lake Berryessa.

The remaining crimes that police attribute to the Zodiac — the attack at Lake Berryessa, the murder of Paul Stine, and the kidnapping of Kathleen Johns — all exhibit even higher degrees of premeditation, so much so that there is little value in rehashing their details. The key takeaway is that the three Southern California crimes and effectively all those perpetrated by the Zodiac in the Bay Area suggest an assailant who planned his criminal activity in advance, invested considerable time and effort into finding victims who fit certain criteria, and struck in environments and under circumstances that facilitated the commission of the crimes.

1.1.4   Sabotage Followed by a Good Samaritan Ruse

Digging deeper into two particular instances of premeditated situational control, the circumstances that allowed Cheri Jo Bates's killer to gain control of her involved a highly effective bit of manipulation. As described earlier, the scheme that the killer employed is perhaps best described as sabotage followed by a Good Samaritan ruse. Specifically, the man disabled Bates's car, and then, once she was unable to start the car, he approached and offered to help. He feigned attempts at fixing the car, all the while knowing his actions would be ineffective. Once the killer had gained her trust, he was able to manipulate Bates into a set of circumstances that soon after led to her death.

The intriguing and relevant point about the killer's manipulation of Bates is that it is very similar to the Zodiac's manipulation of Kathleen Johns. Again, the approach was specifically an instance of automotive sabotage followed by a Good Samaritan ruse. As you may recall from Section 5.2 of *The Zodiac Revisited, Volume 1*, a man began following Johns on Highway 132 near Modesto. He eventually convinced Johns to pull over, at which point he said her rear tire was wobbling. Kathleen accepted the stranger's offer to fix the problem. Unbeknownst to her, he did not tighten the wheel's lug nuts, but rather loosened or removed a critical subset of them. Once Johns tried to drive away, the wheel became completely inoperable. The seemingly helpful man then offered to give her a ride to a nearby filling station. Johns graciously accepted, and her traumatic ordeal began.

Apart from the similarity of the manipulation, the Johns kidnapping is interesting because the perpetrator committed to using this sabotage followed by a Good Samaritan ruse even though it was not an especially good fit. In the case of Cheri Jo Bates, the scheme worked well precisely because the killer was able to sabotage the car without Bates being aware of it. With Kathleen Johns, on the other hand, the kidnapper sabotaged her vehicle while Johns was acutely aware of his presence. Though Johns reacted in exactly the manner her abductor must have hoped she would, many other people likely would have been extremely suspicious of a stranger under similar circumstances.

One reason that explains the perpetrator's desire to use this manipulation despite its potential shortcomings is the idea that he was returning to an approach that had previously worked with Cheri Jo Bates. In other words, the thought of performing the sabotage after making initial contact with the victim was less discomforting than the task of coming up with an alternative, unproven manipulation scheme.

People sometimes casually dismiss this similarity. It is, however, an important one. Other serial killers have been known to craft similar manipulations. Ted Bundy feigned having a broken arm — an act that allowed him to come across as both harmless and in need of help. John Wayne Gacy was known to incapacitate his victims by convincing them to put on handcuffs under the pretense of doing a magic trick. These examples are interesting because, even though the means are entirely different, like Cheri's killer and Kathleen's kidnapper, they all put the victim in a very compromised and vulnerable position. In contrast, the man who murdered Cheri Jo Bates used a very specific type of manipulation. A short time later and a relatively short distance away, so too did the Zodiac.

1.1.5   Coup de Grâce

A common thread running through the two Southern California sweetheart murders is the behavior of the shooter incapacitating the victims from afar and then delivering coups de grâce at point-blank range.   In the case of the Gaviota murders, police theorized that Robert and Linda had made a run for it, probably after a brief struggle with the killer. Shell casings and bloodstains on rocks and sticks suggested that at least one of the victims, probably Linda, had continued to run away after initially being shot.[4] Once the killer had rendered both victims helpless, he approached each of them and fired additional, life-ending, shots.   One of the two doctors who performed the autopsies acknowledged that "... there were some powder burns on the bodies" meaning that they were shot at point-blank range.[12]

Eight months later and nearly 250 miles down the Pacific coast-line, a different scenario with an important similarity played out. A gunman lay in wait, taking advantage of the concealment provided by a makeshift sniper's nest. Once his unsuspecting victims — Joyce and Johnny Ray Swindle — came into position, he opened fire. With the couple gravely injured and effectively unable to move, the killer exited the safety of his cover — roughly 50 feet away — and approached his victims. The gunman then shot Joyce "almost squarely" in the back of the head and Johnny Ray in the left ear, leaving a powder burn.[13,14]

While the Zodiac is not known to have demonstrated this coup de grâce behavior, it's still important. Other evidence connects both of these Southern California crimes with the Zodiac, but the delivery of coups de grâce — as well as other compelling evidence — connects these two so-called sweetheart slayings with each other. More than that, they also paint the picture of a nascent serial killer who was still evolving.

1.1.6   Weapon Caliber and Ammunition

One of the details linking the Gaviota murders to the San Diego homicides was the use of a .22-caliber weapon in conjunction with .22-caliber long-rifle ammunition, albeit the killer in the latter crime used bullets of the hollow-point variety. Interestingly, for his first crime, the Zodiac also chose to use a .22-caliber weapon in conjunction with .22-caliber long-rifle ammunition. In fact, he used the same brand and style of ammunition that the Gaviota murderer had used some five and a half years earlier, namely Winchester-Western Super-X. Table 1.1 details the type of ammunition used in each of the crimes involving a firearm.

As discussed in Section 2.4 of *The Zodiac Revisited, Volume 2*, we know from the Zodiac's crimes that he actively avoided reusing weapons—a choice that gave him control of establishing which crimes should be attributed to him or, perhaps more importantly, made it less clear which crimes should not be attributed to him. The above sequence of events supports the notion of the crimes being committed by a man who was initially predisposed to using .22-caliber, but later, perhaps out of practical necessity, expanded his weapons of choice to other firearms in his personal arsenal.

1.1.7   Military Connections

There is little evidence to suggest that the Zodiac actually served in any branch of the military. However, there is considerable evidence that connects him to various military subjects such as: military dress, firearms, cryptography, and improvised munitions. In the final analysis, we can conclude relatively little based on these connections. For example, did the killer have some tangential involvement with the military through family or friends? Was he merely independently interested in the military? We simply cannot say. However, one of the ways in which this motif does add value is that it provides an additional dimension to compare and contrast the three Southern California crimes against those of the Zodiac.

Date	Location	Victims	Ammunition
June 4, 1963	Gaviota	Robert Domingos Linda Edwards	.22 LR*
Feb. 5, 1964	San Diego	Johnny Ray Swindle Joyce Swindle	.22 LR HP†
Dec. 20, 1968	Benicia	David Faraday Betty Lou Jensen	.22 LR
July 4, 1969	Vallejo	Mike Mageau Darlene Ferrin	9 mm
Sept. 27, 1969	Napa	Bryan Hartnell Cecelia Shepard	.45‡
Oct. 11, 1969	San Francisco	Paul Stine	9 mm
June 19, 1970	San Francisco	Richard Radetich	.38

Table 1.1: Weapon caliber and ammunition used in the extended crimes of the Zodiac that involved a firearm

Likely, the first murder committed by the man who would become the Zodiac took place on a beach in Gaviota. In the commission of this crime, the killer provided the case evidence with its first element of this military theme. During the investigation, police were able to trace the boxes of ammunition that the killer left at the crime

---

* .22-caliber long-rifle

† .22-caliber long-rifle hollow-point

‡ The Zodiac did not fire a weapon during the commission of this crime. However, he used a pistol to control the situation and, at one point, showed Bryan Hartnell the clip in order to confirm that it was, indeed, loaded. Hartnell later, after being shown a variety of ammunition, identified the bullet he had seen in the clip as .45-caliber, although he could not say for sure.

scene — an action that almost certainly indicated his degree of inexperience. Based on the lot number and packaging details, investigators concluded that the boxes had possibly been part of a "brick" (a ten-pack) that someone had purchased through the exchange at Vandenberg Air Force Base.

Chronologically, the next crime was the murder of the Swindle newlyweds in San Diego. In this instance, the military overtones were substantial in that San Diego had, and still has, a large military presence. Moreover, the male victim, Johnny Ray Swindle, was himself a radio operator in the US Navy. This doesn't say much about military connections involving the perpetrator, but, nevertheless, it's a substantive military component.

During the investigation into Cheri Jo Bates's murder in Riverside, detectives discovered a heel print that the killer had left at the scene. Investigators were able to determine that the heel belonged to a shoe that had been manufactured for the military by the Federal Prison Industries Corporation at Leavenworth Penitentiary. More precisely, the particular type of dress shoe had been sold to all branches of the military and, interestingly, was available for purchase at the base exchange of Riverside's own March Air Force Base.[15]

In the case of the Lake Berryessa attack, investigators found numerous footprints left by the perpetrator that they were eventually able to identify as a military shoe called a "wing-walker." Air Force personnel, both military and civilian, commonly wore this type of shoe. Furthermore, these shoes were often sold as surplus. Therefore, though decidedly a military shoe, practically anyone could have purchased a pair. Hence, yet again, there was a connection between a shoe print left at the scene of a crime and commonly available military footwear.

The first two Zodiac crimes were blitz-style attacks that failed to yield any significant ties to the military. However, in the aftermath of the Blue Rock Springs murder and attempted murder, the killer began to demonstrate his penchant for writing taunting letters, and, starting with the very first instance, he exhibited a behavior that is strongly identified with the military, namely the use of cryptography.

While there is nothing definitive that links the Zodiac with *military* cryptography, it is a simple fact that, historically, militaries have been the entities with the largest need for secret communication. Consequently, during the Zodiac era, the military was the organization most actively involved with classical cryptography, both in terms of using it and training people in its use. This level of involvement is clearly evident in the minutiae of the case evidence. For example, Vallejo Police Chief Jack Stiltz enlisted the help of navy cryptographers in an attempt to solve the Zodiac's initial 408 cipher.[16] Furthermore, at the request of the San Francisco Police Department (SFPD), the Army Security Agency (ASA) analyzed the killer's two then-available cryptograms — the 408 which had already been solved and the 340. Interestingly, at one point, the ASA and the army's Criminal Investigation Command (CIC) concluded that the ciphers were constructed by somebody who was "probably trained in cryptography by the U.S. military."[17] Unfortunately, subsequent investigation into the possibility proved fruitless, which, in turn, cast doubt on the claim. In the end, what we can say about the Zodiac's use of cipher is that it provides yet another substantive connection between the killer's persona and the military.

The final Zodiac crime that exhibits a significant military component was the kidnapping of Kathleen Johns and her infant daughter. In a 1998 interview, Johns described the man who abducted her by saying, "He looked military, real clean-cut, extremely clean-cut."[18] She further explained that she had assumed he was in the military because of his "spit-shined" shoes, distinctive glasses, navy-like bell-bottomed pants, and haircut. Clearly the man had invested some amount of effort into projecting a military image, and clearly it had worked.

The killer's ongoing fascination with threatening to blow up a school bus illustrates some level of familiarity with military-based improvised munitions. As detailed in Chapter 6 of *The Zodiac Revisited, Volume 2*, the techniques described by the killer suggest a superficial exposure to the US Army's *Improvised Munitions Handbook,* or possibly an alternative exposure to similar techniques.

Last but not least, the killer's drawing of the annotated compass rose on the Phillips 66 map of the Bay Area and its relationship to nautical and celestial navigation, as described in Chapter 3 of *The Zodiac Revisited, Volume 2,* suggests a possible connection to the US Navy. Certainly, the navy is the branch of service that is most directly involved with such nautical navigation. Furthermore, much of the training associated with the personnel of a naval ship would have provided numerous opportunities for exposure to the subject of celestial navigation. Again, this is not to say that the Zodiac had necessarily been in the navy, only that he may well have had some type of exposure to this branch of the service.

People sometimes make reference to a handful of other possible military connections, such as the military-like page numbering on the Bus Bomb Letter and the use of cipher symbols that resemble naval semaphores. Certainly, there may be something to these observations as well.

1.2   Writing Similarities

Writing similarity, both in terms of form and content, is a compelling way to compare the crimes of the Zodiac against the writing done in conjunction with the murder of Cheri Jo Bates — the only one of the three Southern California crimes that involved any letter writing.

1.2.1   Physical Similarity

Because the author of The Confession typed, through multiple carbon copies, the missive, the only handwriting samples associated with it come from the envelope. Although a copy of the confession was mailed to both the Riverside Police Department and the *Press–Enterprise,* only the envelope from the latter is available in the public domain. Small though it may be, it contains multiple points of commonality when compared with various confirmed Zodiac communiqués.

As a starting point, the writing instrument that the envelope's creator used is the same type preferred by the Bay Area killer, namely a felt-tip pen. The notable difference between the two is the choice of color. In Riverside, the author opted for black, whereas the Zodiac preferred blue. However, the Zodiac did use black when he wrote on the passenger's-side door of Bryan Hartnell's Volkswagen Karmann Ghia.

The next observation to be gleaned from The Confession's envelope is the heavy use of circles instead of dots, a characteristic present in much of the Zodiac's writing and discussed at some length in Section 2.3.1 of *The Zodiac Revisited, Volume 2*. As I noted there, this trait is the result of conscious behavior modification on the part of the Zodiac and was done to provide a subtle dimension of identity verification. In the case of The Confession's envelope (see Figure 1.1), five of the six *i*'s were dotted with circles while the dot on the remaining *i* was omitted altogether. Additionally, a colon contributed two more circles. This conscious alteration being not only present but prevalent in both The Confession's envelope and the writing of the Zodiac is yet another reason to believe that the same person prepared both.

Furthermore, the fact that there are any dotted *i*'s at all is due to a curious choice of letter formation. Specifically, the person who addressed The Confession's envelope chose to use all capital letters with the singular exception of the letter *i*. For the letter *i*, he used the lowercase version of the letter, but he made it just as large as the other capital letters.

Tellingly, if we search the entirety of the Zodiac's communiqués, we can find an instance of the killer writing in precisely the same manner.* On the back of the Halloween Card — where the Zodiac spelled out his four methods of murder and separated each into its

---

*This connection was originally pointed out to me by Douglas Oswell.

Figure 1.1: The envelope from the Riverside *Press–Enterprise* copy of The Confession. The author's use of circles instead of dots is an important idiosyncratic similarity with future Zodiac writing. Image courtesy of Tom Voigt, *zodiackiller.com*.

own quadrant of the card — the content consists of all capital letters with the exception of the letter *i*, which, again was written as an enlarged lowercase *i*. Figure 1.2 shows the relevant part of the card. Again, this type of idiosyncratic letter formation is not the product of an inattentive writer driven by subconscious behavioral predisposition. One arrives at a collection of all capital letters with the exception of enlarged lowercase *i*'s the same way one decides to use circles in place of dots — by way of an explicitly conscious decision.

1.2.1.1   Handwriting Analysis

Handwriting analysis is a bit of a mixed bag when it comes to linking the Zodiac with Cheri Jo Bates's murder. In particular, Sherwood Morrill — California's top handwriting expert during the Zodiac era — spent four days in 1970 analyzing the three taunting letters sent on the six-month anniversary of the Riverside murder and the morbid poem that someone had scrawled onto a Riverside

Figure 1.2: The back of the Halloween Card where the killer used capital letters with the exception of the lowercase *i*'s, exactly as the author of The Confession had done. Image reproduced with permission from the *San Francisco Chronicle* / Polaris.

Community College desk. At the conclusion of his analysis, Morrill determined that the writing was "unquestionably the work of Zodiac," saying:

> *The handprinting scratched on the desk is the same as on the three letters, particularly like that on the envelopes, and this handprinting is by the same person who has been preparing the Zodiac letters that have been received by The Chronicle.*[19]

On the surface, this appears to be an exceptionally damning assessment, and at the time, many people accepted it as just that. However, with the passage of time and the negative publicity surrounding the role that handwriting analysis played in the Toschi debacle (see Section 10.2 of *The Zodiac Revisited, Volume 1*) — especially given Morrill's unwillingness to retract his authentication of the 1978 letter — the strength of this assessment has diminished. In the end, it's fair to say that history has judged Morrill to have been, perhaps, a bit too aggressive in concluding certain handwriting samples were a match to those of the Zodiac. From my perspective, I have serious reservations about the possibility that Cheri Jo Bates's killer wrote the morbid poem, but more for reasons of style and substance than handwriting. This is not to say we should dismiss Morrill's professional opinions, especially as they pertain to the more accepted Zodiac letters. Nor does it mean his opinions are not valuable with respect to the murder of Cheri Jo Bates.

A similar FBI handwriting analysis done in 1974 compared all the Riverside evidence to the handwriting of the Zodiac and tepidly concluded "it was not determined" whether the samples were prepared by the same person due to "variations" in the Riverside writing. The results further stated "nothing of particular handwriting significance was noted."[20]

What we can say, given this set of facts, is that the handwriting from the Riverside evidence does not exclude the Zodiac. Furthermore, in his professional opinion, Morrill was convinced that the Zodiac had authored the six-month anniversary letters and the desk poem. While admittedly not definitive, these professional opinions bolster the argument for a connection between the Zodiac and Riverside.

1.2.2 Content Similarity

Another important aspect of establishing a connection between the Zodiac and Riverside is to consider the relevant writing from a content perspective. When we do this, a striking similarity jumps out. In The Confession, the author used three specific words in very close proximity to one another. Furthermore, he misspelled one of the words, "twiched," by omitting the second *t*. The precise passage reads:

```
SHE SQUIRMED AND SHOOK AS I CHOAKED
HER, AND HER LIPS TWICHED. SHE LET
OUT A SCREAM ONCE ...
```

In the Zodiac's *Mikado* Letter, he used the same three words, again in very close proximity to one another and again with exactly the same misspelling of the word "twitch."

> *Some I shall tie over ant hills and watch them **scream** +*
> ***twich** and **squirm**.*

Digging into this similarity a little more deeply, it's important to point out not only the specific word choice present in these two instances but also the way in which the words are used. In the former excerpt, the killer described observations he allegedly made about his victim as she struggled against the physical assault that claimed her life. In the latter quote, the Zodiac described observations related to hypothetical torture he would inflict upon his "slaves" in the afterlife. In this context, we can come to understand *why* we are seeing these same three words used in close proximity to one another. It's not a coincidence; it's evidence of an underlying motivating factor. These sentiments were described by the same man: a man who took pleasure in observing the pain and suffering of his victims, both in terms of reality — the lines from The Confession — and his motivating fantasies — the sentence from the *Mikado* Letter. In this sense, the final line from the introductory two pages of the *Mikado* Letter is apropos: "I shall have great fun inflicting the most delicious of pain to my Slaves." We're seeing the same words because the same man was writing about the same aberrant psychological pleasure and, in so doing, falling back on the same vocabulary.

As an aside, it's worth pointing out that the *Mikado* Letter was sent in the summer of 1970, a time during which law enforcement was aware of the possible connection between the Zodiac and the Riverside slayer* but several months before Paul Avery publicly reported on the so-called Riverside connection in the *Chronicle*.[22]

As covered in Section 1.3.3 of *The Zodiac Revisited, Volume 2*, there is generally a lack of consensus regarding whether the Zodiac's numerous spelling mistakes were a true indication of his inability to spell or a simple yet effective obfuscation device. Given the complexity and subtlety of some of the killer's language, I come down on the latter side of that argument. If true, the Zodiac's intentional introduction of spelling mistakes into his writing not only makes him look exceptionally challenged in terms of spelling, but it also serves to mask any actual spelling mistakes that he made unintentionally. In other words, we as readers of the letters are unable to distinguish between the spelling errors that the killer intentionally inserted into the letter and the spelling mistakes that he unintentionally made. Given the simple nature of the "twich" misspelling and its appearance in both The Confession and the Zodiac's *Mikado* Letter, I suspect it may well have been the only unintentional misspelling, or perhaps one of a few, that the killer made.

*   *   *

The other word that jumps off the page of The Confession is "shall." This phrasing is formal and somewhat rare in everyday language. Yet, as we have seen, the Zodiac had an affinity for using it, doing so nineteen times throughout his collective writings. The specific line from *The Confession* is:

```
BUT I SHALL CUT OFF HER FEMALE PARTS
AND DEPOSIT THEM FOR THE WHOLE CITY
TO SEE.
```

---

*This possibility was identified at least as early as October 1969.[21]

While there are differences in tone and style between *The Confession* and the letters penned by the Zodiac, I submit that many of the differences are simply because the Zodiac was writing under the guise of a persona. In contrast, the letter describing Bates's murder was likely a much closer reflection of the killer's true self. Nevertheless, a common thread running through both of these written works is a clear sense of grandiosity, which is accentuated through the use of the word "shall." This word is often used in language involving powers that are superior to those of the individual, such as government, law, and religion. In this sense, the killer is conveying that a force more powerful than any individual is driving him, and, hence, individuals are powerless to stop him. The word is likely present in The Confession and the letters of the Zodiac because the same exaggerated sense of power appealed to the disturbed psyche of the same individual.

As intriguing as the phrase "I shall" is, it is not the only way in which the above sentence is potentially meaningful. One consistency across the extended crimes of the Zodiac is a complete absence of sexual assault. The numerous statements that law enforcement made to the media regarding the various crimes almost always pointed out that there was no evidence of sexual assault. The likely explanation for this consistency is that the perpetrator was not motivated by a desire to commit sexual assault. His motivation was simply a psychopathic hatred of young and desirable women and the men with whom they formed relationships. A need to commit sexual assault did not factor into the equation.

In fact, the only hint of a sexual act present in any of the crimes happened in Gaviota when the killer cut away Linda Edwards's bathing suit, exposing her breasts after having stacked her dead body on top of a lifeless Robert Domingos. With no other indications of sexual assault or activity, this action may not have been overtly sexual but rather an attempt to humiliate Linda in death by exposing her body. If correct, this postmortem humiliation through exposure is precisely the sentiment communicated in the above quote from

The Confession. In a very real sense, the murderer of Cheri Jo Bates threatened to do what the murderer of Linda Edwards actually did.

*   *   *

The next similarity between The Confession and the writing of the Zodiac that deserves our attention is the notion of murder and its supporting activities being fun or entertaining. In the Riverside missive, the killer wrote:

> IT WAS A BALL ... BUT THAT WILL NOT
> STOP THE GAME.

The Zodiac expressed a very similar sentiment in his writing, examples include (emphasis added):

> I LIKE KILLING PEOPLE BECAUSE IT IS
> **SO MUCH FUN**[*]

> *In answer to your asking for more details about the **good times** I have had in Vallejo ...* [†]

> *I was at this phone booth haveing some **fun** with the Vallejo cops when he was walking by.*[‡]

Both of these murderers viewed themselves as participating in a competition against law enforcement. Just like Rainsford and the tiger from *The Most Dangerous Game* (see *The Zodiac Revisited, Volume 2*, Section 4.1.1), they viewed themselves as equal, if not superior, adversaries, matching wits against their would-be captors and enjoying every minute of it. This unusual perspective is yet another example of a behavior that other serial murderers could conceivably exhibit but in reality rarely do.

---

[*]Solution to the first third of the 408 cipher sent to the *Vallejo Times-Herald* on July 31, 1969.

[†]Zodiac letter received by the *San Francisco Examiner* on August 4, 1969.

[‡]Ibid.

*   *   *

The final content-based parallel I will draw between the Northern and Southern California crimes has less to do with what was written and more to do with how the author wrote it. Specifically, I am referring to the final notes from the Riverside ordeal and the initial letters of the Bay Area saga. In both cases, a man mailed three different letters in which the content was fundamentally the same, but the writer made minor tweaks to account for the change in recipient.

In the case of Riverside, the letters were very short. The two sent to the *Press–Enterprise* and the Riverside Police Department read simply:*

BATES HAD TO DIE THERE WILL BE MORE

But in the letter sent to Cheri's father, Joseph Bates, the author used a more personal tone, changing "BATES" to "She." He likely made this change for two reasons. First, with Joseph being a member of the Bates family, the author may have felt awkward referring to Cheri through the use of her surname. Second, and likely more importantly, the killer wanted to make the message more personal. Unlike the other two letters, this letter was crafted with the intention of inflicting emotional pain and suffering on the person to whom Cheri was closest. This letter was a type of personal assault, and, therefore, the writer wanted the letter to be more personal than the other two.

A little over two years later, the man who would soon be known as the Zodiac simultaneously mailed three letters, announcing his presence to the world. The recipients of these letters were the three relevant Bay Area newspapers, namely the *Chronicle*, the *Examiner*, and the *Vallejo Times-Herald*. Though more substantive than the Riverside letters, the content between the letters was effectively the same, except for three nontrivial differences:

---

*There were also some differences involving capital versus lowercase letters between the three missives.

1. Each letter included a different third of the 408 cipher.

2. The author mentioned that he was mailing separate parts of the cipher to the remaining two newspapers, which he identified by name.

3. For reasons unknown, the author bestowed upon the *Chronicle* the distinction of an additional sentence that read: "In this cipher is my identity."

What other cases of unsolved murder involved the perpetrator simultaneously mailing three perspective-adjusted communiqués? Apart from these two, I'm aware of no others. At the same time, these two instances were separated by a small amount of time (just over two years) and a reasonably short distance (approximately 450 miles) and were accompanied by an abundance of circumstantial evidence that suggests both were the work of the same individual.

It's also worth pointing out that the media did not report on the Riverside letters at the time of their arrival. In other words, prior to Paul Avery's articles documenting the possible Zodiac-Riverside connection in November 1970, the public was not aware of the Riverside notes. Hence, it would have been impossible for one man to have murdered Bates and write the letters while a different man became the Zodiac and mimicked the notes based on public knowledge. The only way for the Zodiac to have been influenced by the Riverside notes when he wrote his three perspective-adjusted letters to Bay Area newspapers was if he, in fact, was the man who also wrote the Riverside communiqués.

1.3   Behavioral Similarities

The primary behavior linking the murder of Cheri Jo Bates to the Zodiac is the taunting of law enforcement and the general public by way of letter writing to local newspapers. Certainly, there are differences between the Riverside letters and the collection of writings attributed to the Zodiac, including matters of style, tone, and even physical construction. For example, The Confession was typewritten, whereas the Zodiac preferred to hand print his correspondence. However, most would agree that the fundamental goals of these letters were similar; they were intended to instill a sense of fear in the public and a sense of helplessness in members of law enforcement who were tasked with solving the murders.

Beyond this obvious connection, there are a couple more subtle behavioral similarities that link the Zodiac to the murder of Cheri Jo Bates.

1.3.1   Survivor Tormenting

Lurking within the details of some of these crimes is a fascinating thread of commonality. In the case of the Riverside murder, we know Cheri's father received a taunting letter at the six-month anniversary of her death. Interestingly, Kathleen Johns claimed to have received a card from her abductor, and Donna Lass's sister also reported receiving a strange greeting card referencing her sibling, who was missing and presumed dead.

During the Zodiac era, newspapers routinely engaged in the journalistic practice of reporting a person's address when he or she became newsworthy. As an unfortunate consequence, victims of crimes often found their addresses published in the paper. Multiple news articles from the Riverside *Press* reported Joseph Bates's address, which made it exceptionally easy for Cheri's killer to mail the distraught father.[9,10,23]

In a lengthy 1998 interview, Kathleen Johns explained that a San Bernardino newspaper had published her address as part of a story that reported her abduction. Understandably, Johns was very displeased and uncomfortable with the release of this information. She complained to the newspaper, which indicated that it had received the story from the *San Francisco Chronicle*'s Paul Avery, presumably via a wire service.* Johns went on to claim that the following Halloween, she received a Halloween Card very similar to the one the Zodiac had sent to Avery, albeit without any of the customizations present on his card, such as the addition of the pumpkin and the second skeleton (see Figure 5.16 of *The Zodiac Revisited, Volume 1*). Of particular note was the writing in the card, which simply said: "To the lady in the station wagon" — you may recall that Johns's vehicle was a station wagon, a detail that was *not* disclosed in either of the newspaper articles that documented her ordeal.[24,25]

In an unfortunate turn of events, Johns claimed she mailed her card to Paul Avery after conversing with him. Consequently, she did not have possession of the card, and, of course, Avery never mentioned it. Given the level of detail in the story and Johns's conviction when telling it, I feel compelled to believe her. However, not being able to verify parts of the story also suggests that she may have incorrectly remembered some of the details, probably owing to the interview taking place nearly thirty years after the events.

That brings us to Donna Lass's sister, Mary Pilker. In an article that appeared in the *Chronicle* on March 26, 1971, Paul Avery quoted briefly from interviews he conducted with Donna's mother and sister.[26] The two lived in South Dakota, and in his article, Avery mentioned their respective cities. Although the story did not contain either one's street address, from reading the article the killer would have had sufficient information to anonymously acquire the addresses through commonly available means.

A little over three and a half years later — during the 1974 Christmas season — Mary received an eerie, anonymous Christmas card addressed to her personally at her home. The front of the card showed a picture of a snow-covered pine tree in and among other similar trees. As you may recall from Section 7.3 of *The Zodiac Revisited, Volume 1*, Donna Lass was abducted and presumably

---

*Johns provided a very detailed description in her interview. However, I have been unable to find any newspaper articles that match her description.

murdered while living and working in the Lake Tahoe area, a region characterized by pine trees. Inside the card, the manufacturer's message read: "Holiday Greetings and Best Wishes for a Happy New Year," to which the sender added:

> *Best Wishes.*
> *St. Donna & Guardian*
> *of the Pines*

Curiously, the person who wrote the message and addressed the envelope did so using a cursive writing style that looked distinctly different from the Zodiac's hand printing. The card was postmarked December 27 and had been mailed from somewhere in the Bay Area's Alameda County.[27]

All three of these instances paint a picture of a criminal who re-lived the thrill of his crimes by attempting to inflict emotional pain onto those who were most hurt by his original wrongdoing. As we saw with the use of the words "scream," "squirm," and "twich" [*sic*], the man was driven by a desire to make others suffer. What's clear from this evidence of tormenting his victims' survivors is that emotional pain was an acceptable substitute for physical pain. The important element of the man's motivation was the presence of pain; the particular type of pain mattered less.

This behavior provides yet another connection between the murder of Cheri Jo Bates and the Zodiac, and yet another reason to conclude that the two perpetrators were one and the same.

I have often wondered if there may have been other instances of survivor tormenting in the case. This type of contact could have been easily misunderstood, dismissed, or otherwise overlooked. At this point, we probably will never know.

1.3.2   Anniversary Commemoration

Another characteristic behavior found in the Riverside murder and the crimes of the Zodiac is the idea of commemorating certain types of anniversaries with letter writing. With Bates's murder, the killer wrote his three taunting, perspective-adjusted notes and mailed them such that they were postmarked April 30, 1967 — the six-month anniversary of Cheri's death. In similar fashion, two and a half years later, the Zodiac mailed defense attorney Melvin Belli a letter that was postmarked precisely on the one-year anniversary of the Lake Herman Road murders of David Faraday and Betty Lou Jensen.

The final instance of commemoration involved an anniversary of a completely different sort. As discussed in the prologue of *The Zodiac Revisited, Volume 1*, the Zodiac's "My Name Is" Letter was clearly a response to the *Examiner* article in which Dr. D. C. B. Marsh, president of the American Cryptogram Association, challenged the serial killer to construct a cipher that truly concealed his name.[28] The killer mailed the letter two days prior to the six-month anniversary of the article's publication, and, as a result, both the *Chronicle* and the *Examiner* reported news of the letter on the date of the anniversary.[29,30]

The act of letter writing obviously served multiple and varied purposes for the Zodiac; to name a few, it provided the opportunity for taunting, self-aggrandizing, establishing threats, increasing media exposure, and — in the case of the Bus Bomb Letter especially — even simple venting. Some of these purposes were practical, but most, if not all, appear to be born out of a desire to satisfy certain needs in the killer's psyche. What is evident in the above instances of commemorative letter writing is that the author increased the level of satisfaction he experienced by manipulating the timing of the letters. This type of activity required time, effort, planning, and possibly discipline — in each case, the author may have deferred the writing or mailing of the letter in order to achieve an arrival on the given anniversary. This behavior was both substantive, important, and yet another reason to believe that the man who murdered Cheri Jo Bates went on to become the Zodiac.

1.4 Self-Admission

There is one other reason to believe that the Bay Area killer murdered Cheri Jo Bates — he admitted it. Specifically, in his March 13, 1971, letter to the *Los Angeles Times*, he wrote:

> *I do have to give them credit for stumbling across my riverside activity, but they are only finding the easy ones, there are a hell of a lot more down there.*

People tend to dismiss this part of the argument for two reasons. First, the killer was, demonstrably, a liar; there are unequivocal examples of him being untruthful, for example, the ever-increasing murder score and his claim that the 408 solution would reveal his identity. Second, the idea of the killer being truthful, in this and similar contexts, does not sit well with other commonly held views of the Zodiac, especially in terms of the Taking Credit theory.

As explained in Sections 1.3.4 and 1.3.5 of *The Zodiac Revisited, Volume 2*, I do not subscribe to the Taking Credit theory, and I believe that the killer preferred to be honest when his situation did not require dishonesty. In this context and in light of the other supporting evidence, I believe the Zodiac was being honest when he made the above statement. In other words, he killed Cheri Jo Bates, and the combination of the Gaviota and San Diego crimes — at least in part and probably in full — constituted the "hell of a lot more down there."

Furthermore, when the author of The Confession wrote: "she is not the first ...," this was a factually accurate statement. When the same author continued " ... she will not be the last," and the preparer of the three perspective-adjusted, taunting notes wrote " ... there will be more," not only were these factually accurate statements, but they correctly characterized the author as a serial killer who was closer to the start of his murderous career than the end.

1.5   Law Enforcement Recognition

It's important to point out that law enforcement had numerous on-going suspicions that these crimes were connected. They were just unable to prove a connection because proof would have required a conclusive match involving either ballistics, fingerprints, or, more recently, DNA. Of course, the evidence has stubbornly refused to yield such a match.

As noted earlier in this chapter, after the Gaviota murders, Santa Barbara County Sheriff James Webster warned surrounding areas that the "maniacal 'sweetheart slayer' " might surface elsewhere along the coast to prey upon lovestruck couples.[1] When the Swindles were gunned down in San Diego, Webster immediately suspected that the Gaviota killer had done just as he'd predicted. The Swindles were murdered on a Wednesday night. Appreciating the significance of the development, by Friday, Webster had two detectives in San Diego with shell casings in hand. When ballistics concluded that the bullets used in the Gaviota murders did not match those from the San Diego slayings, Webster still maintained his suspicion, commenting: "the manner in which both couples were gunned down on the beach without apparent motive indicates that the same killer may have committed both crimes, getting rid of his old rifle after the first crime."[1] Detectives investigating the Gaviota murders would get sidetracked by a red herring in the form of the "Sandy" suspect — a situation that did not fully resolve itself until eighteen months after the murders when George Gill was finally interviewed and cleared. However, the key point here is that Sheriff Webster's understanding of the killer and his intuition regarding the circumstances were likely right on target. A short time later, the Zodiac would be confounding Northern California law enforcement agencies with a criminal methodology that included never using the same firearm twice. Given these facts, it's a definite possibility that the scenario Sheriff Webster described was precisely what happened.

When the Zodiac emerged in the Bay Area, gunning down a lovestruck teenage couple on a dark and lightly traveled Lake

Herman Road, members of the San Diego Police Department (SDPD) took notice. Within days, the SDPD telephoned the Vallejo Police Department; a letter from San Diego Chief of Police O. J. Roed soon followed in which he provided a synopsis of the Swindle murders and requested a shell casing from the Lake Herman Road murders so a ballistics comparison could be made.[3] However, once again, no physical linkage could be established.

A few months after the Zodiac began his letter writing campaign, and, at about the time he was reaching the pinnacle of his impact, the above pattern repeated itself with the Riverside Police Department (RPD) contacting the Napa County Sheriff's Office, first by telephone and then via written letter.[21] The purpose of the communication was to point out the similarities in the Riverside and Lake Berryessa crimes and to suggest that the same person may have committed both. These events played out just over a year before Paul Avery from the *Chronicle* discovered the possible connection himself and reported it to the rest of the world.[22]

Finally, as documented in the description of the Gaviota murders (see Section 8.1 of *The Zodiac Revisited, Volume 1*), after inheriting the case in 1972 and soliciting information about similar crimes, Santa Barbara County Detective William Baker became convinced that the perpetrator was likely the same man who gravely injured Bryan Hartnell and murdered Cecelia Shepard at Lake Berryessa, otherwise known as the Zodiac.

1.6   The Argument for Southern California

Given the state of the evidence, it's simply impossible to say for certain whether or not the same perpetrator committed all of the extended crimes of the Zodiac. Nevertheless, we should not allow this uncertainty to overshadow the fact that there is an overwhelming amount of physical and behavioral evidence to support the conclusion that a single man was indeed responsible for all of these crimes. Consider the following...

If we accept that Gaviota was *not* committed by the man who became the Zodiac, then we must accept that a different man — who was relatively close to the crimes of the Zodiac, both in terms of time and geographic distance — used the exact same modus operandi that the Zodiac used, including brandishing a firearm, approaching a young couple at the water's edge, and having one tie up the other with precut lengths of rope brought to the scene of the crime. In fact, this similarity was so coincidental that, upon hearing the description of the Gaviota crime, two members of law enforcement familiar with the Zodiac investigation *immediately* recognized the MO as that of the Zodiac. Moreover, there have been zero additional instances of this precise MO in all the years before and since.

In addition, if we accept that the Gaviota and San Diego murders were committed by different people, we must believe that — at a time when stranger murder was still relatively rare in the United States — a man in Gaviota murdered a lovestruck couple using .22-caliber long rifle ammunition; Sheriff Webster recognized the motiveless actions as that of a Sweetheart Slayer; he predicted the killer would resurface to target another couple in a similar coastal area; and, six months later, a different stranger killer did exactly that by murdering a couple on a beach in San Diego using .22-caliber long rifle ammunition by shooting them from afar, approaching, and delivering point-blank coups de grâce, just as the Gaviota killer had done. Then, neither of these two men were ever apprehended.

If we accept that different murderers committed the Gaviota and Riverside homicides, we must believe that, after dragging her lifeless body to the crudely built beach shack, the Gaviota killer abstained from sexually molesting Linda Edwards's body, yet cut away her bathing suit to expose her in death. Then, a short time later, a different killer murdered Cheri Jo Bates, wrote The Confession, and threatened postmortem exposure of a hypothetical victim's "female parts," exactly as had happened in Gaviota.

If we accept that Cheri Jo Bates's murderer was someone other than the man who became the Zodiac, we must believe that, in an era when Riverside had no unsolved homicides on its books, a different man lured Cheri to her death using the same manipulation scheme that the Zodiac would employ a few years later when kidnapping Kathleen Johns, namely automotive sabotage followed by a Good Samaritan ruse. During the commission of Cheri's murder, this different man left an impression of military footwear, just as the Zodiac would do three years later during the Lake Berryessa attacks. Then, after a silence of approximately one month — the same amount of time between Blue Rock Springs and the Zodiac's first letters — this different man also engaged in the rare practice that would become the Zodiac's signature behavior: writing taunting letters to newspapers. And, of course, The Confession that this different man wrote was not just some letter; it was a letter that shared an extraordinary number of characteristics with the writings of the soon-to-be Bay Area killer. In particular, this different man used a felt-tip pen, just like the Zodiac; this different man described his murderous deeds as fun and a game, as the Zodiac would later do (and notably, unlike nearly all other serial killers who communicated with the media); this different man used handprinting that some experts claimed was that of the Zodiac while other experts could not exclude the possibility; this different man used all capital letters with the notable exception of the letter *I*, which he formed using and an oversized lowercase *i*, just as the Zodiac would do; this different man employed a conscious writing alteration whereby he converted dots to circles, as the Zodiac later did; the different man used the same rare phrase that many would come to identify as a curious idiosyncratic trait of the Zodiac: "I shall.... "; and finally, this different man used the words "squirm," "scream," and "twitch" — misspelling the latter as "twich" — in the span of two lines, just as the Zodiac would do and precisely as no other communicating serial killer has ever done, before or since.

Then, six months later, this different man mailed three similar letters with perspective-adjusted content to three different recipients, just as the Zodiac would do two and a half years later. This different man mailed the letters to coincide with the six-month anniversary of his victim's death, just as the Zodiac mailed the "My Name Is" Letter to coincide with the six-month anniversary of Dr. D. C. B.

Marsh's public "dare" and analogous to how the Zodiac mailed the
Belli Letter to commemorate the one-year anniversary of his first victims' deaths. Moreover, this different man sent one of the three letters
to Cheri Jo Bates's father — the only person with whom she lived at
the time of her death — as a cruel act designed to inflict psychological
pain and suffering into the life of the man who had been closest to the
young woman, just as the evidence shows that the Zodiac would later
do. Finally, when law enforcement and the Riverside community un-
dertook the impressively creative step of reconstructing the night of
Cheri's murder, minute for minute, it's just a coincidence that people described the singular person for whom there was no accounting
using the one word that people would later consistently choose to
describe the Zodiac: "heavyset."

As for the Zodiac himself, we must accept that upon learning of
the suggestion that he was responsible for the Riverside death, the
man — who proactively denied responsibility for one murder* and
abstained from taking credit for three others when the press had all
but made the association† — readily admitted to a murder committed
by somebody else and openly stated he had killed more people in the
region when, in fact, he had not.

Meanwhile, fate has been exceptionally kind to the Zodiac in that
all of the Southern California crimes that have come to be associated with him have remained unsolved for five decades and count-
ing, just like the rest of his crimes. The real murderers of the five
Southern California victims — including Cheri Jo Bates's killer who
said: "She is not the first and she will not be the last" — have faded
into the woodwork, never to be heard from again. These men, who
were afflicted with a mental condition that drove them to the point
of taking another human being's life in a very premeditated manner, suddenly disappeared into society in such a way that they never
again drew attention to themselves. Neither future criminal activ-

---

*The Zodiac denied responsibility for the SFPD Park Station bombing.
†The Zodiac attempted to take credit for neither shooting taxicab driver
Charles Jarman nor stabbing Deborah Furlong and Kathy Snoozy.

ity, nor communications made in confidence, nor inadvertent action have betrayed their respective identities. Unlike the cases of Charles Jarman, Deborah Furlong, and Kathy Snoozy — where the media invited the Zodiac to associate himself with the crimes, but he refused — the Southern California crimes have remained unsolved.

The alternative to this convolution is simple: there was no different man.

Somewhere in his late twenties, this single killer — motivated by a pathological hatred of attractive women and the men who are able to form intimate relationships with them — targeted a symbolic couple who was otherwise unknown to him. He was inexperienced, made mistakes, lost control, but got away with the crime. Soon after, driven by the same motivation, he made his way to San Diego. Learning from his mistakes, he operated more efficiently this time. Surprised by Sheriff Webster's instant recognition of his crime, the man laid low for a bit before resurfacing. He decided to change his modus operandi and focus on the primary source of his hatred — women — in the form of a lone stranger. After the murder of Cheri Jo Bates, his continuing evolution took another step when he started experimenting with post-offense communication by writing The Confession and commemorating the six-month anniversary of the murder with his three perspective-adjusted notes. At some point between 1967 and 1968, he moved from Southern California to the San Francisco Bay Area where he conceived of and brought to life his murderous persona: the Zodiac. Through the commission of his crimes and the writing of his communiqués, he established the numerous connections between himself and his previous crimes. He eventually evolved to the point where he faded away — but not before he truthfully claimed responsibility for the death of Cheri Jo Bates and the other murders via the statement "there are a hell of a lot more down there."

This alternative to the previously described litany of improbabilities is a straightforward, logical, consistent, and much more likely criminal evolution.

Notes

1. Arthur Berman, "Honeymooner Killings Called Maniac's Work," *Los Angeles Times*, February 8, 1964, 1.

2. "Couple Found Slain on Secluded Beach," *Los Angeles Times*, June 7, 1963, 1.

3. O. J. Roed of the San Diego Police Department to the Vallejo Police Department, December 31, 1968.

4. Barney Brantingham, "Sacramento Youth Cleared in Slaying," *Santa Barbara News-Press*, June 11, 1963, A–1.

5. "Slayer of Lompoc Pair Deliberately Reloaded," *Los Angeles Times*, June 9, 1963, I1.

6. Pliny Castanien, "Double Killing Probe Turns to 7 Bullets," *The San Diego Union*, February 12, 1964, A–19.

7. "Detectives Sift Leads in Slayings," *The San Diego Union*, February 9, 1964, A–15.

8. Elliott Leyton, *Hunting Humans: Inside the Minds of the Real-Life Hannibal Lecters*, London: John Blake Publishing Ltd, 2001, p. 50.

9. "RCC Coed, 18, Slain on Campus," *The Press*, October 31, 1966, A1.

10. "Police File 352-481 Gets Thicker; Cheri Bates Murder Case Month Old," *The Press*, November 30, 1966, B1.

11. Nancy L. Slover, "Crime Report Supplement: Case No. 243 146," July 8, 1969, Accessed November 25, 2020, *http://zodiacrevisited.com/book/vpd-1969-07-08*.

12. "Two Lompoc High Seniors Are Slain," *Santa Barbara News-Press*, June 6, 1963, A–1.

13. Stevens, Seargent E. C., "Officer Report," May 21, 1964, San Diego Police Department, 1.

14. Pliny Castanien, "Psychopathic Sniper Hunted in 2 Slayings," *The San Diego Union*, February 7, 1964, A–17.

15. Melvin H. Nicolai, "Bureau of Criminal Identification and Investigation Report," January 22, 1971, Accessed November 25, 2020, *http://zodiacrevisited.com/book/doj-1971-01-22*.

16. "Coded Clue in Murders," *San Francisco Chronicle*, August 2, 1969, 4.

17. *Zodiac, Extortion, OO: Sacramento*, Internal Correspondence (Teletype), Federal Bureau of Investigation, San Francisco Field Office, January 22, 1970.

18. Johns, Kathleen, interview by Johnny Smith and Howard Davis, "H. J. N. Terprises, Inc.," January 1, 1998, audio recording.

19. Paul Avery, "Zodiac Link Is Definite," *San Francisco Chronicle*, November 17, 1970, 2.

20. *Zodiac, Extortion*, Report of the FBI Laboratory: File No. 9-49911, Federal Bureau of Investigation, Washington D.C., May 2, 1974.

21. L. T. Kinkead of the Riverside Police Department to Earl Randol of the Napa County Sheriff's Office, Voigt, Tom, October 20, 1969, p. 1, Accessed November 25, 2020, *http://zodiacrevisited.com/book/zk-riverside-memo-1*.

22. Paul Avery, "New Evidence in Zodiac Killings," *San Francisco Chronicle*, November 16, 1970, 1.

23. Yvonne Eggers, "Widowed Father Waits in Vain for Slain Daughter," *The Press*, October 31, 1966, A3.

24. "Rode with Zodiac, Woman Claims," *San Francisco Examiner*, March 23, 1970, 4.

25. "Woman Says Zodiac Killer Captured Her," *The Modesto Bee*, March 23, 1970, A–1.

26. Paul Avery, "Zodiac Hints of a Body Near Tahoe," *San Francisco Chronicle*, March 26, 1971, 1.

27. Howard Davis, "The 1974 Christmas Card and Envelope," Accessed November 25, 2020, *http://zodiacrevisited.com/book/zmc-christmas-card*.

28. "A Challenge to the Zodiac," *San Francisco Examiner*, October 22, 1969, 1.

29. Paul Avery, "Zodiac Sends New Letter — Claims Ten," *San Francisco Chronicle*, April 22, 1970, 1.

30. Don Branning, "'Zodiac' Boasts of 10 Killings," *San Francisco Examiner*, October 22, 1970, 18.

Reconsidering the Letters

Letters are among the most significant memorial a person can leave behind them.

Johann Wolfgang von Goethe
German poet, playwright, and novelist
1749–1832

It's impossible for an author to communicate through writing without revealing aspects of him or herself in the process. Be it the explicit thoughts consciously articulated or the latent impressions unwittingly woven into the words, what we write and how we ultimately chose to do it says much about who we are and why we feel compelled to interact with the world around us. Even when we set out with the intention to deceive, how we choose to do it says something. It's impossible to rid our words of every last telltale sign that, in some way, betrays our dishonesty.

It is with these thoughts in mind that we turn our attention to the roughly 3,000 words that exist precisely because the Zodiac chose to write them. As well as anything, the ideas embodied by these words paint a picture of our unknown subject. The numerous pieces of physical evidence that have been available to law enforcement for so many decades are well-known entities. Notwithstanding any miraculous development in forensic science, the evidence will be tomorrow what it was yesterday. And since, after so long a time, no one has managed to parlay the evidence into the elusive fugitive's identity, it's unlikely to happen anytime soon. But the written words of the killer and the ideas that they communicate are not bound by the same constraints. As seen in elements of the Zodiac's methodology, we may continue to develop a better understanding of the killer's written words and the thoughts that he intended to convey. These concepts are considerably less well-defined and, as such, represent our best chance of associating a name with the man who, thus far, has been known to the world only as the Zodiac.

In the following sections, I review the most meaningful parts of each communiqué and attempt to make sense of them in light of what we've learned about the killer.

2.1   The Confession | November 29, 1966

The first observation to make regarding The Confession is not about its content, but rather its construction. As we know, the killer typed the letter. But what's not obvious on first inspection is that the way he typed the letter says something about his knowledge of typing. Being old enough to have endured a year of typing class in high school — on actual typewriters — I'm familiar with the process of learning to type. One rule from that era is that there was always supposed to be two spaces between sentences. As a consequence, anyone formally trained to type during this time frame would automatically, almost subconsciously, hit the space bar twice at the end of every sentence.

In the case of The Confession, the killer sometimes used two spaces and sometimes used one. In particular, he used two spaces between the first fourteen sentences.* Then he transitioned to using

---

*The exception is between sentences twelve and thirteen, where the man used zero spaces.

a single space between the remaining twenty-nine sentences. These circumstances suggest that the man had some kind of exposure to typing; he knew that there were supposed to be two spaces between sentences. Yet, he likely did not have formal training because if he had had such training, he would have subconsciously and consistently used two spaces. It appears that at the beginning of the letter, the man was paying close attention to the spacing between sentences. But as he continued, his attention drifted elsewhere[†] and he reverted to his default inclination of using a single space.

These circumstances are reminiscent of the killer abandoning sequential assignment partway through the 408 cipher, as described in Section 5.2.2 of *The Zodiac Revisited, Volume 2*. That behavior, in conjunction with the omission of a word between sections two and three, suggested that the killer may have taken a break during the construction of the cipher. The same possibility exists with The Confession. Perhaps the man wrote the initial part of the letter, paying close attention to the spacing between sentences, and then took a break. Upon returning to the task, he may have simply forgotten that he had intended to use two spaces between sentences.

Moving on to the content of The Confession.

SHE WAS YOUNG AND BEAUTIFUL.

This concise sentence precisely described the target of the killer's hatred: (1) female, (2) young, and (3) beautiful. It's no accident that this was the first sentence of The Confession — it's the essence of the whole confession in five words. The man was lashing out at society, targeting its young and beautiful women. Some dysfunction in his life had prevented him from forming normal, intimate relationships with members of the opposite sex. He blamed society; he blamed

---

[†]The transition to single spaces happens right before the sentence "IT WAS A BALL," which effectively starts the discussion of how the killer ensnared and murdered Cheri Jo Bates. It's easy to imagine that the man may have derived a perverse sense of enjoyment from reliving the murder through this retelling of events and, hence, was distracted from sentence spacing.

women (notably, he didn't blame himself), and he was exacting his revenge on both.

> BUT NOW SHE IS BATTERED AND DEAD.

This was a declaration of power that served a psychological need present in the mind of the killer. He was saying something equivalent to: she was young and vibrant, then she crossed paths with me, and now she's "battered and dead." He clearly took pleasure in making this type of statement. It feels like he envisioned himself as an arbiter of death, passing judgment upon all the people he encountered, deciding who lived and who died.

> SHE IS NOT THE FIRST AND SHE WILL NOT
> BE THE LAST.

Apart from the fact that my beliefs require this statement to be true, there's also a certain consistency to it. A person writing in the aftermath of his first and only murder likely would focus solely on the task of convincing his audience he was responsible for the murder. Needlessly taking credit for nonexistent previous murders would only serve to detract from his credibility at a time when he's trying hard to establish it. So the statement really serves little purpose unless it is, indeed, true. Either way, most analysts would agree if the letter writer is not caught, he will go on to kill again.

> I LAY AWAKE NIGHTS THINKING ABOUT MY
> NEXT VICTIM.

This statement is undoubtedly true and, honestly, unremarkable. Serial killers are driven by compulsive fantasies of past and future actions.

> MAYBE SHE WILL BE ...

It's hard to read too much into the specific examples he gave. It's impossible to prove or disprove the statements. Perhaps they have some basis in fact in terms of being fantasies created about real people that existed at some point in his life, perhaps not. Almost certainly, these women were not other residents of Riverside, even though that seems to be the implication. As likely as not, the women were complete fabrications of the killer's imagination, constructed solely to add an element of realism to the author's threats.

BUT MAYBE IT WILL NOT BE EITHER.

Adding to the power motif, the writer wanted to make it clear that he was in control. Again, he viewed himself as Death, if not God, deciding who lived, who died, and what did and did not happen.

BUT I SHALL CUT OFF HER FEMALE PARTS
AND DEPOSIT THEM FOR THE WHOLE CITY
TO SEE.

The first point of interest in this statement is the archaic use of the word "shall," which would soon come to be a common vocabulary choice for the Zodiac starting with his very first letter less than two years later. The verb "shall" seemed to be important to the killer because it conveys a sense of authority above and beyond that of the person doing the speaking or writing. Often laws or other formal documents use "shall" because they are empowered by government or other authorities. Religious doctrine often uses the word, the Ten Commandments being the principal example; in this case, of course, God is the authority behind the message. Again, because the killer wanted to establish himself as equivalent to Death or God, he used this language to elevate the perception of his self-assigned authority.

The other aspect of this statement concerns what the man claimed he was going to do. He could've made any claim here and said anything he wanted to, no matter how vile and how depraved. History has many examples of serial killers who have done disturbing things to their victims, both premortem and postmortem — albeit many of the examples were yet to happen at the time of this letter. With very little imagination, we can envision threats of sexual assault using vulgarities that are a common part of many people's lives. But we don't get that here. The man referred to "female parts," which is a phrase one can imagine people using in casual professional or academic settings if such a topic were to come up; in other words, it's not profane in the least. It's almost as if he felt the need not to be offensive while he made this depraved threat. He wanted to make a shocking statement about what he was capable of doing, but the best he could muster in reference to his hypothetical victim's anatomy was "female parts."

Finally, the way in which the man said he was going to defile the victim was through what can best be described as postmortem humiliation. He was not going to rape her. He was not going to torture her. Rather, he was going to humiliate the victim by exposing her "female parts" after she's dead. Honestly, this is a strange threat. Of all the things he could possibly do, this is what he chose? This statement reveals an aspect of the symbolic revenge that motivated this murderer. It was not enough to kill. He wanted to kill and then humiliate. One can easily imagine that the man was thinking in these terms because he felt he'd been humiliated by women throughout his life. He'd been humiliated by his inability to form meaningful relationships with women, and now he wanted to even the score not only by killing the type of young and beautiful women with whom he could only fantasize about having a relationship but also by making them feel in death the way he'd been forced to feel in life.

MISS BATES WAS STUPID.

It's curious that he chose to refer to Cheri as "Miss Bates." Normally, this is an indication of unfamiliarity or respect. We can obviously rule out respect since the man wantonly murdered her and made the claim that she was stupid; unless, of course, we assume that he was being sarcastic, which is possible but doesn't feel right. The problem with the name suggesting unfamiliarity is that the author claimed familiarity with Cheri later in the letter when he said he was "making her pay for the brush offs...." I believe this was partially an attempt at depersonalizing the victim by using the unfamiliar tone and a subconscious indication of the real relationship he had with Cheri, which is to say he did *not* know her. Cheri was a symbolic victim, which is why the killer ultimately didn't care what he called her. If this crime had really been a personal one, committed by someone who was close enough to the victim to be brushed off, he likely would have called her Cheri.

The claim that she "was stupid" is just an unsurprising indication that the killer needed to feel superior. He needed to feel superior to his victim, Cheri; he needed to feel superior to women more generally; he needed to feel superior to society. In fact, this sentence is an introduction to a section of the The Confession in which the killer explained how brilliant he was in laying his trap for Cheri. This whole section primarily served to assert the author's superiority; a secondary consideration was to establish the author's identity as the murderer. Truth be told, Cheri did the same thing that millions of other young women would have done if confronted with similar circumstances in 1966 America. It was just unfortunate, that in so doing, she ensnared herself in the web of a man who was dedicated to the task of ending her life.

SHE WENT TO THE SLAUGHTER LIKE A LAMB.

This statement is almost certainly a reference to the biblical passage " ... he is brought as a lamb to the slaughter ... ," which suggests the killer may have been a practicing Christian at some time in his life.* Also, this indirect reference to God could be seen as a means of reinforcing the notion that the killer viewed himself as God.

From an alternative perspective, the assertion could be viewed as a continuation of superiority and power motifs. In other words, the

---

*Isaiaah 53:7

man's ruse was so good that Cheri participated in it willingly until it was too late. From the author's point of view, he was omnipotent and Cheri was as helpless as a lamb being led to slaughter.

> SHE DID NOT PUT UP A STRUGGLE.

This statement continues the same power assertion. Given the relative positioning of this statement, I interpret the "struggle" to be a symbolic reference to the events leading up to Cheri's death, not an actual physical struggle once the violence started. Clearly, Cheri did put up a physical struggle as evidenced by the debris found under her fingernails and Detective Yonkers' description of the death scene as: "... so churned up it looked like a tractor had been over the ground."[1]

> BUT I DID.

Again, the implied "struggle" is the mental planning and the formulation of the ruse that enabled the killer to achieve control over Cheri. By making this statement, the killer was basking in what he perceived to be his own brilliance.

> IT WAS A BALL.

This psychopathically remorseless characterization of murder as fun or a game is effectively the same as what would be seen from the Zodiac in the Bay Area less than three years later.

> I FIRST PULLED THE MIDDLE WIRE FROM
> THE DISTRIBUTOR.

This is the primary line that identifies the author of the letter as the murderer of Cheri Jo Bates. Multiple articles had mentioned that the killer had tampered with the vehicle so it wouldn't start, but none had specifically mentioned pulling the middle wire,[*] which was the key part of what he had done.[3,4]

Beyond verifying the identity of the killer, this statement and much of the subsequent description were designed to show how clever the author was — how he was a master manipulator. Again, this air of self-congratulatory description is similar to what would later be seen from the Zodiac, for example, when he explained how he attached a flashlight to his firearm. And, honestly, the author of The Confession was an intelligent person. He clearly had significant automotive knowledge, an understanding of human nature, and he'd obviously invested considerable time and thought into the construction of his ruse.

> THEN I WAITED FOR HER IN THE LIBRARY
> AND FOLLOWED HER OUT AFTER ABOUT TWO
> MINUTS.

This is improbable. Spending time in the library would have increased his level of risk unnecessarily. More likely, he simply approached Cheri under the guise of someone who just happened to be walking by. In this passage, he was probably suggesting he came from the library to reinforce the image that he fit in as a student or the type of person one would expect to find in a college library.

> I THEN OFFERED TO HELP. SHE WAS THEN
> VERY WILLING TO TALK TO ME.

There are, undoubtedly, certain threads of truth woven into this self-serving, fictionalized account of what happened. From my perspective, the key to understanding The Confession is viewing Cheri

---

[*]Zodiac researcher Michael Morford pointed out that there was actually one lesser-known article that mentioned the "... wire from the coil to the distributor had been pulled."[2] People with automotive knowledge would have recognized the described wire as the "middle wire" of the distributor. While this find is undeniably interesting, it doesn't substantively change the situation.

as a symbol or a proxy for what the killer was really attacking. This outrage of Cheri being willing to talk to the man when she seemingly stood to benefit from the conversation was likely a real reflection of what motivated the killer. At this point in time, the man was probably in his early thirties. Throughout his adult life, he almost certainly felt that beautiful women wanted little or nothing to do with him under normal circumstances. From the killer's perspective, the fact that these women would behave differently when in need of help was evidence of their duplicitous nature and further proof that he was justified in his beliefs.

```
I TOLD HER THAT MY CAR WAS DOWN THE
STREET AND THAT I WOULD GIVE HER A
LIFT HOME.
```

It's curious that the author chose not to mention the feigned attempts at fixing the vehicle, which he clearly made based on the greasy palm prints found on the car. Nevertheless, this described scenario is unlikely. Multiple friends pointed out that Cheri's car was her pride and joy. She always locked it. If she really left the vehicle with the expectation of getting a ride home, she probably would have locked the car and taken the books that she'd checked out of the library. She did neither. More than likely, she willingly left her vehicle as the result of the killer employing some type of different, but unknown, ruse.

```
WHEN WE WERE AWAY FROM THE LIBRARY
WALKING, I SAID IT WAS ABOUT TIME.
SHE ASKED ME "ABOUT TIME FOR WHAT".
I SAID IT WAS ABOUT TIME FOR HER TO
DIE.
```

Again, the author is taking creative liberties with what actually happened. The library reopened at 6:00 p.m., closed at 9:00 p.m., and the attack happened around 10:15 p.m. No matter how we slice it, there is a large amount of time unaccounted for, and reality is inconsistent with the casual description provided by the author. These circumstances call into question the veracity of the dialogue described by the killer. It's just as likely that the dramatic dialogue is a fictionalized account of what happened, crafted for the purposes of telling the story.

```
I GRABBED HER AROUND THE NECK WITH MY
HAND OVER HER MOUTH AND MY OTHER HAND
WITH A SMALL KNIFE AT HER THROAT.
```

Given the author's willingness to bend the truth, there's really not much we can say about this description. Maybe it's accurate, or maybe it's not. We do know that the knife was a small knife. But that fact was well known, and it provided little additional insight into the murder.

```
...HER BREAST FELT VERY WARM AND FIRM
UNDER MY HANDS, BUT ONLY ONE THING
WAS ON MY MIND.
```

This is an interesting and explicit acknowledgment of the rather rare dynamic that ties all the Southern California murders together and also links them to the majority of the Zodiac crimes. Specifically, this murder was a sexually motivated assault that lacked any real component of sexual assault. The killer chose the victim because she was young and beautiful. He chose her because of who she was and what she represented to him. He chose her because of the sexual inadequacy he felt in relation to women like Cheri. But he had no intention of sexually assaulting or abusing her. With Cheri's death, the killer was making a statement to society. He felt compelled to make the statement because of sexuality and the injustices that women like Cheri had caused him. But the statement spoke of his need for violence and power not sex.

```
MAKING HER PAY FOR THE BRUSH OFFS
THAT SHE HAD GIVEN ME DURING THE
YEARS PRIOR.
```

This is the one line that many people believe implies the killer knew Cheri. As discussed earlier, the Riverside PD took this line quite literally and, hence, focused their efforts on a suspect who was well known to Cheri. Clearly, I believe this was a mistake. The killer did not know Cheri and likely had never seen her before the night he saw her at the RCC Library.

In fact, I suspect this line is an instance of intentional misdirection on the part of the author. From Gaviota to San Diego to Riverside, we see an evolution in false-motive establishment. In Gaviota, there was no motive evident in the murders, apart from the symbolism of the victims. In San Diego, the killer took Johnny Ray's watch and wallet, thereby creating the misguided suggestion that robbery was a possible motive. The crime was obviously disproportionate to the motive of robbery, and law enforcement saw through it immediately — especially given Sheriff Webster's keen insight. Regardless, the killer manipulated the crime scene in order to suggest a possible, alternative motive. Here in The Confession, with the above sentence, the killer flat-out told the Riverside PD his supposed reason for killing Cheri. He gave them a reason to believe something other than his true motive, which was symbolic revenge. Unfortunately, they seem to have been all too willing to believe it.

```
SHE SQUIRMED AND SHOOK AS I CHOAKED
HER, AND HER LIPS TWICHED. SHE LET
OUT A SCREAM ONCE AND I KICKED HER
HEAD TO SHUT HER UP.
```

As detailed earlier in Section 1.2.2, this sentence is a strong indication that the man who wrote The Confession was the same man who authored the Zodiac letters.

> I PLUNGED THE KNIFE INTO HER AND IT
> BROKE. I THEN FINISHED THE JOB BY
> CUTTING HER THROAT.

It's unclear whether or not the knife actually broke during the attack. Different people have reported different things on this point. In response to The Confession, Riverside Police reported they "had no evidence that the knife ... broke during the struggle."[5] In the end, it doesn't really matter much. Even if there was no indication that the knife broke, it's possible it may have broken in a way that did not leave telltale evidence. Regardless, there is enough information in the letter to convince most objective people that the author was, indeed, the man who murdered Cheri. Therefore, the question of whether or not the knife broke and whether or not the author was being honest about it is moot.

> I AM NOT SICK. I AM INSANE.

This is a strange statement and one I've thought about for quite some time. While it's impossible to know precisely why the author made it, I can suggest one reasonable interpretation.

Insanity is a designation constructed by society. People get together and agree on what it means to be sane and, likewise, insane. Though underlying mental illness is a real phenomenon that afflicts populations in a manner similar to sickness, especially in the extreme, governments and legal systems — in other words, people, not nature — determine where to draw the line and whom to deem insane. Even the same governments and legal systems, over time, will change their definitions of what constitutes insanity.

As an aside, the currently accepted definition of insanity in the United States — from a layman's legal perspective — involves the question: did the person understand the difference between right and wrong? Again, this definition and its application are both dynamic and have evolved in the decades since Cheri's killer secretly typed out The Confession. It would be wrong to suggest the author intended his statement to be interpreted against the backdrop of our modern definition. Interestingly, however, if we were to argue from the modern perspective, we would arrive at a conclusion diametrically opposite of the killer's assertion. The man was undoubtedly afflicted with some form of mental disorder and, therefore, sick. However, he also provided clear evidence that he knew his actions were wrong, so therefore he was also sane. But all this matters little because it's not the distinction the killer was trying to make.

Contrary to insanity, the notion of sickness is more of a natural phenomenon. People may collaborate to name and classify disease, but they don't decide where to place its boundaries in a manner analogous to insanity. Of course, there are vast degrees of illness that span the spectrum from symptomless to acutely terminal. However, in a fundamental sense, you're either sick or you're not. And if you are sick, it's because your body has fallen victim to some form of a naturally occurring environmental interaction or genetic manifestation.

With this understanding in mind, the killer was likely saying that he was not abnormal from a natural perspective; he was only living outside the rules that society had imposed. He would probably argue that death and murder are a normal part of existence for all species on Earth and that our desire to eradicate murder from civilization is tantamount to denying an elemental component of who we are as human beings. The killer would claim that *he* was the one brave enough to follow the rules set forth by nature, if not his view of God. On the other hand, it is *we*, the rest of law-abiding society, who are timidly living in denial of our intended existence, afraid to violate rules that others have imposed on us in order to achieve some silly, altruistic desire to make the world a better place for everyone.

BUT THAT WILL NOT STOP THE GAME.

The author characterized his need to commit murder and taunt law enforcement and the public as something entertaining, similar to the Zodiac's actions a few years later. Again, this is important because it stands in stark contrast to the behavior of most other serial murderers.

> THIS LETTER SHOULD BE PUBLISHED FOR
> ALL TO READ IT.

This statement suggests an evolving signature aspect of the killer. No longer was he content to read about his crimes passively. From this point forward, he needed to actively participate in the protraction of his crimes through written communication. He needed to increase the coverage his crimes received by taunting law enforcement and the public. And finally, he needed to feel the excitement of knowing an audience was reading the words that he himself had written.

> IT JUST MIGHT SAVE THAT GIRL IN THE
> ALLEY.

In addition to writing to newspapers and demanding publication — as the Zodiac did — the author of The Confession couched his demand for publication in terms of it preventing future action, much the same way the Zodiac did with his first letters, the Dripping Pen Card, and the Dragon Card.

Again, the "girl in the alley" was likely a symbolic construction, partially intended to make the threat feel local and real. The killer likely had no connection to Riverside other than having chosen to commit a murder there.

> BUT THAT'S UP TO YOU. IT WILL BE ON
> YOUR CONSCIENCE. NOT MINE.

This is an intriguing denial of responsibility. In essence, the killer was saying: "I've told you what I am; if you choose not to act, it's your fault, not mine." In some sense, the author was asking the powers that be to stop him through the act of publication. But, at the same time, he was very much unapologetic for the person he was and the actions he had taken. Of course, he clearly didn't have a conscience in the way most people do.

> YES I DID MAKE THAT CALL TO YOU ALSO.
> IT WAS JUST A WARNING.

The Riverside Police Department acknowledged receiving what it described as "a number of crank phone calls."[5] Unfortunately, the content of any such calls was never made public, and their significance was apparently not appreciated at the time. The experience of having made these calls may have factored into the way the Zodiac later approached his phone calls. In fact, he may have chosen to call in the immediate aftermath of his crimes precisely because he thought they would be taken more seriously. In other words, by calling about events before news of those events had been made public, the probability of the person on the receiving end of the phone call thinking it was a crank call would be virtually nonexistent.

> BEWARE ... I AM STALKING YOUR GIRLS
> NOW.

Just as the first statement of the letter was especially meaningful, so too was the last. Notice how the killer was not threatening just any women; he was threatening "your girls" — "your sisters, daughters, and wives." It was not just the act of murder that was driving the killer; it was the idea of murdering women about whom people cared. In the intervening decades, we've seen numerous killers who serially murder prostitutes because they are easy victims. Typically having few strong relationships with family and friends, the disappearances of these women often go unnoticed or unreported for days, if not longer. It was no coincidence that the author of The Confession was not interested in this type of easy victim. He didn't want women who were carving out an existence on the fringes of society. He wanted young beautiful victims who seemed to have it all. He not only relished the symbolic revenge he exacted from his victims, he also enjoyed the hurt it inflicted on all the people who knew and loved them. This element of his behavior was why the man was motivated to send the six-month anniversary note to Cheri's father. Having the ability to create pain and suffering in the lives of others gave the man a clear sense of power and a perverse satisfaction.

2.2 First Letters | July 31, 1969

As mentioned previously, the three letters postmarked July 31, 1969, were mostly equivalent, except for some perspective adjustments based on the recipient of the given letter. There was, however, one significant difference between the three — the discussion regarding the cipher.

In the letter to the *Vallejo Times-Herald*, the Zodiac wrote:

> *Here is a cipher or that is*
> *part of one. the other 2 parts*
> *have been mailed to the S.F.*
> *Examiner + the S.F. Chronicle*
> *I want you to print this*
> *cipher on your front page by*
> *Fry Afternoon Aug 1-69. ...*

The verbiage in the letter to the *Examiner* was exactly the same, with the newspapers changed accordingly. But in the case of the *Chronicle*, the wording was different.

> *Here is part of a cipher the*
> *other 2 parts of this cipher are*
> *being mailed to the editors of*
> *the Vallejo times + SF Exam*
> *iner.*

I want you to print this cipher
on the front page of your
paper. In this cipher is my
identity.

There are several points of interest here. First, the claim that the cipher contains the author's identity was only made in the *Chronicle*'s letter. Second, a precise reading of the passage raises a curiosity. When the author wrote: "In this cipher is my identity," the word "cipher" was being used in exactly the same context as the previous sentence where the Zodiac demanded that the paper publish the cipher. In other words, the author was not referring to the cipher as a whole, but rather to the one third of the entire cipher that was sent to the *Chronicle*. This interpretation may explain why the extra statement was not included in the letters to the two other newspapers.

Following this logic a bit further, it's interesting to note precisely what the Zodiac claimed in the letter to the *Chronicle* and precisely what he denied in the decryption of the cipher. Specifically, in the former, the killer wrote that the cipher contained his identity whereas in the latter, he stated: "I will not give you my name." While one's identity and one's name are similar and related concepts, they are not exactly the same. Of course, identity is a more general idea that could be established through various means. For example, a person can identify him or herself through initials, a social security number, a username (more recently), etc. A name, on the other hand, is a very specific form of identification.

Taken together, it is possible that these two statements — "In this cipher is my identity" and "I will not give you my name" — are both true. For example, the Zodiac's initials could be included within the text or the cipher symbols of the *Chronicle*'s one third of the 408 cipher. Alternatively, he might be using a different form of identity, a form that is not as obvious. The unfortunate aspect of this observation is that we will likely never know one way or the other, unless the

Zodiac is unquestionably identified through other means. Nevertheless, this possibility provides a consistent explanation for the facts as we know them.

2.2.1 A Notable Difference

As discussed, there are noteworthy similarities between the letters in the Cheri Jo Bates homicide case and the Zodiac letters of July 31, 1969. However, something else to consider is the way in which The Confession differs from these Zodiac letters. In particular, the author of The Confession mailed two copies — one to the Riverside Police Department and one to the *Press–Enterprise*. This choice was likely motivated by the killer simply considering whom he wanted to have read the letters, namely law enforcement and the public.

But by the time the Cheri Jo Bates story had run its course in the newspaper, the author of the letters had likely concluded that sending his communiqué to the police had added little value. Because law enforcement had access to anything sent to the newspaper, sending the letter to the police was redundant and unnecessary. Moreover, both letters were taken into custody and processed by the California State Crime Lab. The key to having the letter published was sending it to a newspaper.

Throughout the Zodiac's letter writing campaign, which began two and a half years after The Confession was written, the killer never bothered writing to the police directly. Once again, we find behaviors from the Cheri Jo Bates murder and the Zodiac crimes that we can interpret as a logical evolution.

2.3 The Debut of the Zodiac Letter | August 2, 1969

People may find it surprising that the Zodiac decided to send his next letter to the *Examiner* and not the *Chronicle*. But, by this time, the *Examiner* had shown the killer favorable treatment on two separate occasions. In the case of the Lake Herman Road murders, the

Examiner not only reported on the story a day ahead of the *Chronicle*, but it did so on the front page. The *Chronicle* relegated the story to page A10.[6] Reporting on the Blue Rock Springs shootings had been the same between the two newspapers because the only story appeared in the joint Sunday edition.[7] With the news of the Zodiac's initial letters, the *Examiner*'s reporting again preceded that of the *Chronicle* by a day.[8,9]

So by the time the killer sat down to write the initial letter in which he referred to himself as the Zodiac, the precedent was clear: the *Examiner* had provided better coverage, both in terms of timing and placement. Therefore, the killer's likely reasons for choosing to write to the *Examiner* are understandable and logical. The more interesting question is: Why did he never again write to the *Examiner*?

*   *   *

This is the Zodiac speaking.

Although all aspects of the Zodiac's persona and methodology were almost certainly in place by the time of the Lake Herman Road murders, the killer still chose to defer the use of his self-assigned moniker — and this ominous introduction — until his second letter. One possible reason for doing so is that, in the interest of prolonging his newsworthiness, he was attempting to hold back some amount of information that the news-consuming public would find intriguing.

> *In answer to your asking for*
> *more details about the good*
> *times I have had in Vallejo,*
> *I shall be very happy to*
> *supply even more material.*

Vallejo Police Chief Jack Stiltz's ploy to goad the killer into writing yet again in the hopes of procuring additional physical evidence and perhaps the author's identity had been well publicized in the newspapers and other media outlets. The killer's air of extreme cordiality was a clear mechanism for taunting law enforcement. The attitude in this introduction feels as if the killer was saying: "I know what you want, and I know why you want it. But I'm so good that I'm going to give it to you anyway."

> *By the way, are the police*
> *haveing a good time with the*
> *code? If not, tell them to cheer*
> *up; when they do crack it*
> *they will have me.*

This was simply additional straightforward taunting. Of course, predictably, solving the 408 did not yield the killer's identity. Still, the author enjoyed setting the erroneous expectation that it would.

The killer's use of the word "code" here is noteworthy. As discussed in Section 5.1.2 of *The Zodiac Revisited, Volume 2*, what the killer sent is technically not a code; in general terms, it's a cryptogram, but more specifically it's a cipher. This use of the word "code" is one of the few instances where the killer uses the technically inaccurate term.

> *I did not leave the cene*
> *of the killing with squealing*
> *tires + raceing engine as described*
> *in the Vallejo paper. I drove away*
> *quite slowly so as not to draw*
> *attention to my car.*

These statements are referencing an article in the July 6, 1969, edition of the *Vallejo Times-Herald*, which described details from an earwitness who was clearly George Bryant, the son of the Blue Rock Springs Golf Course caretaker. The relevant section of the article includes:

> *"This took place shortly after midnight," said a detective sergeant. "He [the witness] couldn't hear any voices. But*

*he heard the car take off at a high rate of speed, peeling
rubber and cutting corners. He wasn't sure, but he thought
it was headed toward the freeway."[10]*

Both Bryant and surviving victim Mike Mageau independently
described the killer as leaving the scene of the crime at a high rate
of speed. Given these descriptions, especially the calmly observed,
disinterested observations of Bryant, this scenario was likely correct.
To be sure, the case evidence offers other examples of the murderer
acting in a deliberate and self-disciplined manner consistent with the
letter's described behavior. Nevertheless, in this instance, the killer
was either being deceitful (which is unlikely since the purpose of the
letter was to further establish his identity via information) or his per-
ceptions of his own actions during the perpetration of the crime were
inaccurate, likely as a result of the mental dynamics associated with
the moment.

> *The man who told the police
> that my care was brown was a
> negro about 40-45 rather shabbly
> dressed. I was at this phone
> booth having some fun with the
> Vallejo cops when he was walking
> by. When I hung the phone up
> the dam X@ thing began to
> ring + that drew his attention
> to me + my car.*

Neither the *Chronicle* nor the *Examiner* had mentioned that the
killer was driving a brown car. However, the *Vallejo Times-Herald*
mentioned it repeatedly. In the first two articles covering the Blue
Rock Springs shootings, the description was given without mention
of the source.

Saturday, July 5, 1969

Officers at the scene broadcast an alert for a young, heavy-set, white male adult, riding in a brown automobile, as wanted for questioning in the shooting.

This may or may not have been the person who made the anonymous call to police headquarters.[11]

Sunday, July 6, 1969

The officers are looking for a stocky young white man who was driving a brown car.[10]

However, in subsequent stories, the newspaper revealed that the source was Mike Mageau.

Monday, July 7, 1969

The interrogation was brief, but Mageau at least was able to describe the killer's car, Rust said....

He tumbled to the ground, however, and saw the slayer's car as it sped away.

The killer's car bore a California license [plate], Mageau told Rust.[12]

Tuesday, July 8, 1969

He described the killer as short and [heavyset], and said he was driving a brown car similar to Mrs. Ferrin's brown 1963 Corvair.[13]

Given the direct references to the quotes by George Bryant, we know that the killer had read the Sunday, July 6 edition of the *Vallejo Times-Herald*. However, because he incorrectly identified the person who told police that his car was brown, claiming it was "a negro about 40-45 rather shabbily dressed," we can assume he did not read the editions of the newspaper where the source was reported to be Mike Mageau, namely July 7–8. From the content of his letters and his narcissistic personality, we know that the killer had an insatiable appetite for news articles about himself. If he would have had access to the newspaper, he would have read those stories. Therefore, we can conclude that he did not regularly have access to the *Vallejo Times-Herald*.

Interestingly, July 6 was a Sunday. We know that the Zodiac was predisposed to carrying out his murderous deeds on weekends, suggesting the possibility that the killer held a conventional Monday-through-Friday type job. Perhaps the killer was comfortable obtaining a copy of the Vallejo newspaper on weekends, but he was unable to during the week. Finally, if the killer actually lived in Vallejo, as many have suggested, he likely would have had a subscription to the *Vallejo Times-Herald* and would have been fully aware of every story having to do with the murders. These facts and their circumstances are yet more evidence that the killer did not live in Vallejo.

Regarding the incident involving the "negro about 40-45 rather shabbily dressed," the Zodiac was likely describing an actual happening. If the killer had not learned that Mageau was the source for the "brown car" description, he probably would not have expected that the young man could have identified his car, given the circumstances of the attack. Furthermore, by the time the killer phoned the Napa Police Department following the Lake Berryessa attack in September 1969, he had modified his behavior, choosing to leave the handset dangling instead of hanging it up. Clearly, he learned a lesson following the Blue Rock Springs attack, as described in the letter, and subsequently modified his behavior. Unfortunately, the witness described by the Zodiac was never identified. In all likelihood, he never came to understand the significance of the seemingly innocuous events that he witnessed.

> *Last Christmass*
> *In that episode the police were*
> *wondering as to how I could*

> *shoot + hit my victoms in the*
> *dark. They did not openly state*
> *this, but implied this by saying*
> *it was a well lit night + I could*
> *see the silouets on the horizon.*
> *BullShit that area is srounded*
> *by high hills + trees.*

Here again the Zodiac was referring to a passage from the *Vallejo Times-Herald*, this time from an article published December 23, 1968.

> *[Solano County Sheriff's Sgt.] Lundblad explained the killer needed no artificial lighting for accuracy in shooting the girl, since she was running on a plateau and her body was silhouetted against the sky.*[14]

The letter continued:

> *What I did*
> *was tape a small pencel flash*
> *light to the barrel of my gun.*
> *If you notice, in the center*
> *of the beam of light if you aim*
> *it at a wall or celling you will*
> *see a black or darck spot in*
> *the center of the circle of*
> *light aprox 3 to 6 in. across.*
> *When taped to a gun barrel,*
> *the bullet will strike exactly*
> *in the center of the black*
> *dot in the light.*

As others have noted before me, this does appear to demonstrate a certain level of mechanical ingenuity on the part of the killer, assuming he came up with this idea himself. It's interesting to note how prevalent laser-sighted firearms have become in the intervening years. In fact, even toy guns are now sometimes equipped with such laser sights.

> *All I had to do*
> *was spray them as if it was*
> *a water hose; there was no*
> *need to use the gun sights.*

The killer seems to have lost himself in the self-satisfaction he experienced from writing this description. The use of the word "them" is imprecise in that the flashlight mechanism only would have applied to Betty Lou. David Faraday was shot behind the ear at point-blank range.

> *I was not happy to see that I*
> *did not get front page cover-*
> *age.*

The Zodiac had demanded that each of the three recipient newspapers publish its respective third of the 408 cipher on its front page by August 1, 1969. Strictly speaking, the *Examiner* was the only newspaper that abided by the killer's deadline. Yet, it relegated the story to page 4 and did not include the cipher. As the recipient of the second letter, the newspaper had been rewarded for meeting the assigned deadline. Nonetheless, the author clearly felt compelled to point out and admonish the newspaper for not adhering to all his demands.

2.4   The Stine Letter | October 13, 1969

> *I am the murderer of the*
> *taxi driver over by*
> *Washington St + Maple St last*
> *night,...*

Cab driver Paul Stine was murdered at the corner of Washington and Cherry Streets. However, the man who committed the murder requested a destination of Washington and Maple, one block east. When Stine arrived at the original destination, the passenger apparently instructed him to drive forward one additional block.

These facts suggest that the killer planned the murder with knowledge of the intersection of Washington and Maple Streets. When the Zodiac ended up one street past Maple, he likely did not know the name of the street and further did not feel inclined to figure it out. If nothing else, this scenario appears to indicate the killer was not especially familiar with the Presidio Heights neighborhood.

> *... to prove this here is*
> *a blood stained piece of his*
> *shirt.*

The Zodiac had played along with Vallejo Police Chief Stiltz's claims that the author of the July 31 letters might not be the actual perpetrator of the Lake Herman Road and Blue Rock Springs crimes. As requested by Stiltz, the killer followed up with his August 4 letter to the *Examiner* — a letter that was also met, at least initially, with some degree of skepticism. These events clearly had an impact on the Zodiac. Instead of dictating the terms of the discussion, he found himself reacting to the dictates of law enforcement in order to establish something that, in his mind, should have been self-evident — that he was who he said he was.

The way these events played out clearly established a need, in the mind of the killer, to come up with a better mechanism for verifying his identity. The new mechanism needed to irrefutably prove that only the Zodiac could have committed the given crime. As a result, the killer came up with the idea of removing a bloodstained piece of the victim's clothing, which he felt should verify his identity in no uncertain terms. Gone would be the need to include numerous and subtle details of the crime. Gone would be the need to react to law enforcement's contrived quibbling. One small piece of fabric and nobody would even suggest that he was not who he said he was. He was right.

> ... *I am the same man*
> *who did in the people in the*
> *north bay area.*

This statement possesses a certain ambiguity. Was the killer referring to the Lake Berryessa attack, the two Vallejo-area attacks, or all three? Given that he'd already written and claimed credit for the Vallejo attacks, it would seem more likely that he was referring to the only other attack that had happened since his previous letters, namely Lake Berryessa.

Also noteworthy is the choice of verb in this statement: "did in." The killer often referred to himself as the "murderer," as he did in the opening statement of the Stine Letter. Author David Van Nuys, as part of his analysis of the Zodiac letters in his book *"This Is the Zodiac Speaking"*, pointed out that the killer used this self-ascribed label in very open and unapologetic terms.[15] In other words, the killer made no attempt to hide behind euphemistic rationalizations. Instead, he was openly boastful. So when the killer changed his verb of choice from "murdered" (or something similar) to the less ominous "did in," it raises the question: what purpose does it serve?

One good explanation for the choice of words is that the Zodiac was, indeed, referring to the attack on Bryan Hartnell and Cecelia Shepard, and, he chose the slightly different phrase "did in" to account for the fact that Hartnell survived. A common definition of the phrase "to do in" is "to kill." However, it can also mean "to injure gravely." Hence, the killer may have found it useful to take this less precise phrase and use it to paint both victims with the same broad strokes, even though it resulted in less shock value. This single statement certainly sounds better than something along the lines of "I am the same man who murdered one person and seriously injured another in the North Bay area." Of course, it's also possible that the Zodiac chose the phrase for these same reasons, but he intended for it to apply to all six of his previous victims, including survivors Bryan Hartnell and Michael Mageau.

The term "North Bay" is a subject in and of itself. From a definitional perspective, the North Bay region of the San Francisco Bay Area embodies Solano, Napa, Marin, and Sonoma Counties. Therefore, technically, all three of the previous attacks were in the North Bay region. However, designations such as North Bay and East Bay are more informal in everyday use. With Vallejo being near the border of the two regions, people often associate it with the East Bay rather than the North Bay, especially since traveling to Vallejo from San Francisco requires crossing the Bay Bridge in an easterly direction. In fact, in one interview, Inspector William Armstrong of the SFPD described how he'd read about the "Cipher Killer" striking in the East Bay prior to the Stine murder.[16]

In the end, the killer's reference to the phrase "North Bay" may have had less to do with the subtleties of Bay Area geography and more to do with him responding directly to a newspaper article. On October 1, ten days before Paul Stine's murder, the *Examiner* ran a story that began:

> *A psychotic killer police say brutally slays females for sexual gratification is loose in the North Bay today.*[17]

A few paragraphs later, the story continued:

> *Four of the persons stalked and slain lived in the North Bay region.*

In the final analysis, the killer's statement remains ambiguous; we are unable to know for certain whether he was referring only to the Lake Berryessa crime or rather all three of his prior crimes. But given the killer's penchant for reading and responding to newspaper articles and the otherwise appropriateness of the reference, the strongest probability is that he was referring to all three of these crimes.

2.5   The Dripping Pen Card | November 8, 1969

The nearly simultaneous mailing of this greeting card, which included the 340 cipher, and the subsequent letter that was postmarked a day later probably came about due to the lead time required to construct the cipher. Crafting the length-appropriate content, encrypting it based on the constraints imposed by the cipher, and carefully laying out the finished product would have required considerable time and effort. Based on the hostility contained within the Bus Bomb Letter, the killer clearly had a considerable amount of pent-up frustration by the time he mailed the Dripping Pen Card.

> *This is the Zodiac speaking*
> *I though you would need a*
> *good laugh before you*
> *hear the bad news*
> *you won't get the*
> *news for a while yet*

Precisely what the killer meant by "bad news" remains just as much a mystery today as it was when the editorial staff at the *Chronicle* read it for the first time so many decades ago. Notably, the statement seems to imply that a force outside the control of the killer was preventing communication of the bad news. One reasonable interpretation that dovetails nicely with this idea is that the bad news was part of the content encrypted by the 340 cipher. Hence, law enforcement would not receive the bad news until they deciphered the cryptogram. Unfortunately, without a viable solution to the cipher, we have no way of knowing if this is a correct interpretation or not. Nevertheless, it is, in my estimation, a likely possibility.

> *PS could you print*
> *this new cipher*
> *on your front page?*

With this statement, the killer's previous outright demands for publication had given way to this almost polite question that all but conceded his relative position of weakness. All that's missing here is the inclusion of the word "please" or perhaps the phrase "if it's not too much trouble."

> *I get awfully lonely*
> *when I am ignored,*
> *so lonely I could*
> *do my **Thing**!!!!!!!*

Predictably, the killer's slip into near politeness was short-lived as he immediately returned to threatening more violence.

This thought, as communicated by the killer, is a bit odd. The killer's desire to act out his murderous deeds was at least partially motivated by feelings of loneliness. On the other hand, public acknowledgment in the form of front-page newspaper coverage helped provide a sense of connectedness that somehow alleviated the need to act out against the society from which he felt disconnected. While this may be either plainly untrue or contrived, it was, nevertheless, a curious way to couch the retaliatory threat.

> *Des July Aug*
> *Sept Oct = 7*

This postscript was the first occurrence of what will soon evolve into the killer's continual taunting through a running score that was clearly intended to represent his murder victim count. There are two problems with this so-called score. First, the correct victim count at the time of the letter was five not seven. Second, it correctly accounts for each month with the exception of August — none of the known murder victims had been killed in August.

As discussed in Section 4.1 of *The Zodiac Revisited, Volume 1,* some have interpreted these two facts to mean that the killer was implying he was responsible for the highly publicized and heinous murders of Deborah Furlong and Kathy Snoozy — two San Jose teenagers who were savagely murdered in August 1969.

One major problem with this belief — and the Taking Credit theory (see *The Zodiac Revisited, Volume 2,* Section 1.3.4) — is an article published in the *Examiner* on October 1, 1969.[17] Ten days before the murder of Paul Stine, the article all but attributed the murders of Furlong and Snoozy to the Zodiac. Given the killer's penchant for reacting to content in both the *Chronicle* and *Examiner,* it's a near certainty that he read the story. Moreover, the article was the same one that characterized the killer's victims as being from the "North Bay," the exact phraseology the killer would use just two weeks later in the Stine Letter, further suggesting that he'd read the October 1 *Examiner* article. Yet, the Stine Letter — which mentioned other victims from the North Bay, albeit ambiguously — made no mention of Furlong and Snoozy, neither directly nor indirectly.

To be sure, the Zodiac undoubtedly enjoyed the speculation that he may have been responsible for the murders of Furlong and Snoozy. But it's doubtful that he was explicitly including them in his murder count.

2.6   The Bus Bomb Letter | November 9, 1969

Within the Zodiac's entire collection of correspondence, the Bus Bomb Letter is unique. Be it the rambling six pages, the killer's announcement of his intention to "change the way" he perpetrated his crimes, the initial occurrence of the bus bomb diagram, or the cryptic *X*'ed Zodiac symbol, the content of this letter provides significant insight into the mind of the murderer.

This is the Zodiac speaking

Ever the media-savvy participant, this introductory phrase had become a highly effective mechanism that the serial killer used to brand his persona. Continued inclusion of the phrase within his letters was an absolute must.

> *Up to the end of Oct I have*
> *killed 7 people.*

Not surprisingly, this assertion was exactly the same as the postscript from the Dripping Pen Card. In some sense, the killer was picking up right where he'd left off with the previous day's correspondence.

> *I have grown*
> *rather angry with the police*
> *for their telling lies about me.*

Upon the receipt of the Stine Letter, San Francisco's powers that be had a grave and unpleasant situation with which to contend. A known serial killer who had verifiably struck within city limits was openly and unabashedly threatening to murder the most defenseless and cherished members of the community — children.

In the span of a few sentences, the Zodiac had left city officials with no good options. Withholding the threat from the public would have amounted to professional suicide in the event that the killer actually made good on his threat. On the other hand, disclosing the threat to the public was certain to result in widespread panic. Ultimately, there really was little question about what to do; given the responsibilities of their respective offices, city leaders were obligated to disclose the threat, which they did.

For his part, Chief of Inspectors Martin Lee settled on a strategy that he felt would partially allay the public's fears upon learning of the killer's threat. That strategy was to paint the killer in an incompetent and ineffectual — not to mention unflattering — light. Perhaps nowhere was the outline of this strategy more evident than in an article published by the *Examiner* a week after Paul Stine's murder.[18] In the article, California Attorney General Tom Lynch and Chief of Inspectors Lee offered assessments of the killer that were at opposite ends of the spectrum. Lynch urged the killer to give himself up, saying:

> *We will see that he gets help and that all his rights are protected. He obviously is an intelligent individual.*
> *He knows that eventually he will be taken into custody so it would be best that he give himself up before tragedy is written in blood.*

On the other hand, Chief of Inspectors Martin Lee labeled the Zodiac a "clumsy criminal, liar, and latent homosexual."

Much of the content of the Bus Bomb Letter was intended to be a refutation of the arguments and characterizations made by Lee. Although other members of law enforcement certainly contributed to the displeasure that the Zodiac was experiencing, there is little doubt that the person intended to bear the brunt of the killer's diatribe was Martin Lee.

The killer's use of the euphemism "rather angry" is interesting. Every aspect of this letter indicates that the killer was seething, yet he described himself as "rather angry." This choice of words might be viewed as a linguistic counterpart to what survivors described as the killer's trait of talking in a monotone. Just as he disallowed the tone of his voice to convey his true emotions, so too did he disguise his true feelings through the use of euphemistic language.

> *So I shall change the way the*
> *collecting of slaves. I shall*
> *no longer announce to anyone.*
> *when I comitt my murders,*
> *they shall look like routine*
> *robberies, killings of anger, +*
> *a few fake accidents, etc.*

Here we have the formal acknowledgment of the change in approach that had begun with the previous-day's greeting card and its postscript, which was clearly designed to confuse the question of how many people were victims of the Zodiac.

From the killer's perspective, the police had violated the rules of the game. The man likely felt he deserved to be treated as an equal adversary — a relationship much like the mutually admiring Rainsford and his tiger prey from *The Most Dangerous Game*, as discussed in Section 4.1.1.2 of *The Zodiac Revisited, Volume 2*. By publicly humiliating the killer, the police — with special emphasis on Chief of Inspectors Lee — had violated this adversarial relationship between the killer and those who sought to bring him to justice. And since law enforcement was violating the rules of his game, the most appropriate response the killer could conceive of was to institute a rule change of his own.

There is evidence suggesting that from the very beginning of his Bay Area killing spree, the man planned to evolve into a bogeyman-like persona that maximized his terroristic impact by introducing uncertainty into various aspects of his crimes. The most notable example of this was that he never used the same firearm twice. The thought of the public constantly asking itself "was that the Zodiac?" in response to the city's never-ending litany of crimes must have provided the man with an ongoing sense of perverse satisfaction. Nevertheless, the disrespect the killer felt as the result of Lee's and the SFPD's actions likely served to hasten and perhaps intensify the bogeyman transformation.

> *The police shall never catch me*
> *because I have been too clever*
> *for them.*

By this time, investigators, reporters, elected officials, and newspapers alike had all ventured into the role of prognosticator by predicting the eventual apprehension of the Zodiac — a typical example is the quote from State Attorney General Lynch as noted in the article quoted on page 74. Here, the killer appeared to be objecting to such predictions. Likely, the choice of the word "never" was specifically chosen to negate the commonly used notion that the killer would eventually be caught.

> *1 I look like the description*
> *passed out only when I do*
> *my thing, the rest of the time*
> *I look entirle different. I*
> *Shall not tell you what my*
> *descise consists of when I kill*

Both the *Chronicle* and the *Examiner* covered Lee's enumeration of what he believed to be the killer's mistakes.[18,19] The above point was in response to Lee's claim that the killer allowed himself to be observed. In the *Examiner*, the comment was reported as follows:

> *Lee noted Zodiac had allowed himself to be viewed by at least three witnesses to murder and that two surviving victims of his murderous attacks will be able to identify him when the inevitable capture occurs.*

The facts surrounding the physical description of the Zodiac suggest that there may have been an element of truth to the killer's claim that he used some form of disguise. We know that the composite of the Zodiac was widely circulated not only within San Francisco but throughout California and literally across the United States. Furthermore, people were willing to report suspects based solely on their physical similarity with the drawing. One FBI memo in particular from the time frame sheds light on the post-Stine environment in which the Zodiac continued to conceal his identity.[20] Less than a month after the SFPD released the first composite drawing of the killer, two separate people notified law enforcement that a Yosemite National Park employee bore a strong resemblance to the fugitive. Yosemite is approximately 150 miles from San Francisco — close in relative terms but far enough away to escape the intensity that gripped the Bay Area. Police investigated the individual and established that he was not the Zodiac; the man just had the misfortune of resembling the most sought-after criminal in the country. In a similar incident toward the end of October 1969, police in Las Vegas arrested and held a twenty-six-year-old man for no other reason than he looked like the police sketch of the Zodiac. The suspect remained in custody until he was cleared of wrongdoing on the basis of fingerprints and handwriting samples.[21]

Apart from the human-interest aspect of these anecdotes, the stories are valuable in that they serve to illustrate the extent to which people were actively reporting potential suspects to law enforcement. Yet, throughout this period of intense public scrutiny, the killer managed to maintain his anonymity. Then, just five months after the Bus Bomb Letter, Kathleen Johns — a woman who had never even heard of the Zodiac before she had the misfortune of encountering him — immediately and without hesitation identified the fugitive as her abductor, later describing the identification as "plain as day."[22] These facts, taken together, suggest that the killer may have indeed employed some means of manipulating his appearance.

Speculation as to the exact nature of the disguise is likely a pointless endeavor. The possibilities span the spectrum from relatively simple and subtle to outlandish and extreme. Without additional information, we are forced to accept the position that we just don't know.

> *2 As of yet I have left no*
> *fingerprints behind me contrary*
> *to what the police say*
> *in my killings I wear trans -*
> *parent finger tip guards. All it*
> *is is 2 coats of airplane cement*
> *coated on my fingertips — quite*
> *unnoticible + very efective.*

Here the killer continued his point-by-point refutation of Lee's list of alleged mistakes. Again, from the *Examiner*:[18]

> *Lee noted the slayer almost certainly had left his marks among a mass of fingerprints found in the Yellow Cab where taxi driver Paul Stine was shot to death here last Saturday.*

It's difficult to fully understand what the Zodiac was intending to accomplish with the above-mentioned statement. Much of the evidence suggests that the killer was relatively unconcerned with the possibility of leaving fingerprints and palm prints. Investigators found prints on letters, in the two phone booths that the killer used, and at the Paul Stine crime scene — including the so-called bloody fingerprint (see Section 3.2 of *The Zodiac Revisited, Volume 1*). In fact, the killer's lack of concern over leaving behind his prints appears to be one of his defining characteristics. Even so, laboratory technicians have had little success in matching the fingerprints with one another.

Hence, the killer's claim is tenuous. With his intentions unclear, we can only speculate as to what he hoped to accomplish via this statement. Perhaps he was attempting to turn the tables on police — Martin Lee in particular — and portray them as incompetent or, to use Lee's word, "clumsy." Perhaps the Zodiac just wanted to refute Lee's point, even though it was a valid one. Or perhaps the killer was just trying to confuse the issue.

If we specifically consider the audience aspects of this letter, we find there are three separate audiences embodied within the content. The later section labeled "must print in paper" was clearly written for the public. While the Zodiac was certainly not surprised that the *Chronicle* published other portions of the letter, his explicit demand made it clear that he would have been satisfied if the paper had only printed the identified section. The remainder of the letter oscillated between two perspectives, one in which the author was ostensibly communicating with the staff of the *Chronicle*, and the other in which he was addressing the police directly.

The above quote from the letter, as with all of the previous content, was directed at the staff of the *Chronicle*. With this perspective in mind, the killer may have been intending to cast a shadow of a doubt over the quality of evidence possessed by law enforcement. In other words, perhaps the killer was intending to influence the *Chronicle's* perspective on the matter.

Regardless of his motivation, the description of the rudimentary technique used to allegedly outmaneuver police undoubtedly satisfied the killer's need to illustrate his cleverness and technical knowledge. Whether or not the killer actually used the technique is another question that's difficult to answer. Again, with law enforcement's confidence in fingerprints acquired from the letters and crime scenes, we are forced to conclude that, at best, his use of the technique was neither consistent nor complete. Reconciling all of the known information, the killer may have used the technique to exercise some amount of control over which fingerprints he was leaving on an occasion-by-occasion basis.

> *3 my killing tools have been bought*
> *en through the mail order out-*
> *fits before the ban went into*
> *effect. except one + it was*
> *bought out of the state.*

In this portion of the killer's letter, he's referring to the fact that both the *Chronicle* and the *Examiner* had documented the efforts of law enforcement to identify him through gun registrations. The *Examiner*, however, had been significantly more dramatic in its coverage. On Monday, October 20, the newspaper published a story that included a front-page headline: "Gun Best Zodiac Killer Clue." The story documented that only 143 9 mm weapons had been sold in San Francisco during the preceding three years. Moreover, each sale had required an application, and detectives were reviewing the handwriting on the applications for similarity to that of the Zodiac.

Two days later, the *Chronicle* followed up on the story:

> *The search for three guns was pressed yesterday throughout Northern California. Gun dealers were being questioned about purchases of .22-caliber and 9-mm handguns, and ammunition for such weapons. Signatures on gun registration forms were being compared with handwriting on notes authored by Zodiac.*[23]*

However, by this point, detectives were offering a much more stark assessment of the tactic's potential:

> *Investigators don't feel Zodiac will be found this way.*[23]

The same article touched upon the ban to which the killer referred.

> *Until new Federal gun laws went into effect earlier this year, many foreign-made 9-mm. models could be purchased through the mail from dozens of outlets advertising in as many magazines.*[23]

Of tangential interest, in this same article police disclosed ballistics analysis that had corrected an erroneous belief. Investigators initially assumed that the 9 mm weapon used at Blue Rock Springs was the same 9 mm weapon used to murder Paul Stine. In fact, the killer had used two different 9 mm weapons.

> *So as you see the police don't*
> *have much to work on. If you*

San Francisco Chronicle. Newspaper index by Bell & Howell Co. Reproduced with permission of Newspaper Indexing Center, Micro Photo Division, B via Copyright Clearance Center.

> *wonder why I was wipeing the*
> *cab down I was leaving fake clews*
> *for the police to run all over town*
> *with, as one might say, I gave*
> *the cops som bussy work to do to*
> *keep them happy.*

Many people consider the fingerprint with traces of blood found on Paul Stine's cab to be one of the most significant clues in the entirety of the case evidence. The killer left this fingerprint on an area of the cab that three young witnesses saw him wiping down.

Although somewhat counterintuitive, if the killer had absolute confidence that his fingerprints were not on file in any database, he may well have actually felt comfortable leaving such evidence behind. Doing so would have enabled law enforcement to connect him to the crimes if he was apprehended. But as long as he alluded law enforcement, he had nothing to worry about. In this sense, a fingerprint could be considered a "fake" clue — not an invalid clue; rather a valid, but ultimately unusable, clue. And certainly, one could characterize law enforcement's ongoing need to compare potential suspects against the available fingerprints as busywork.

> *I enjoy needling*
> *the blue pigs.*

While taunting and derisive, the Zodiac's previous letters had avoided outright ridicule and name calling. In fact, much of the author's previous content was characterized by a notable third-party-observer type of dispassion. However, starting with this statement, the killer began operating under a new set of rules that included an overt contempt of the police. Again, from the killer's perspective, law enforcement's actions — Martin Lee's in particular — were disrespectful and unforgivable, and now the killer was intent upon responding in kind.

*Hey blue pig I
was in the park — you were useing
fire trucks to mask the sound
of your cruzeing prowl cars. The
dogs never came with in 2
blocks of me + they were to
the west + there was only 2
groups of parking† about 10 min
apart then the motor cicles
went by about 150 ft away
going from south to north west.*

Starting at the beginning of this section, the author shifted the target audience away from the staff of the *Chronicle* and began directing his comments unambiguously to the police. And once again, based on the content, the brunt of this dialogue was intended for one person — Chief of Inspectors Martin Lee. In fact, the singular nature of the introductory phrase, "Hey blue pig," actually provides clear evidence that the author was addressing an individual member of law enforcement.

In the media, Lee had explicitly and repeatedly labeled the Zodiac a liar, citing as evidence the killer's claim that he had remained in the area around Julius Kahn Park immediately following Paul Stine's murder:

"His boast of being in the area we were searching while we searched is a lie," declared the chief of inspectors.
"We had the whole area flooded with lights. We had seven police dogs and a large number of patrolmen

---

†One could argue that the word "parking" is actually "barking" because the leftmost line of the letter extends upward like a *b* and downward like a *p*. Rather amazingly, the sentence starts out describing dogs and ends up discussing motorcycles. With the ambiguous word right in the middle, either possibility makes sense. Nevertheless, "parking" is probably the right word because the killer appears to have overwritten the *p* part of the uncertain letter, suggesting that was his true intention.

searching tree by tree and bush by bush. The dogs are the best in the country.

"A mouse couldn't have escaped our attention," said Lee.

He noted the Zodiac letter ... failed to mention the dogs and floodlights and proves "he wasn't anywhere in the vicinity."[18]

When Lee was made aware of the Zodiac's above counterargument, he colorfully described the killer's claims as "poppycock."[24]

The interesting point to keep in mind with this section of the letter is that the killer did not demand that it be published. In other words, although the *Chronicle* did publish this part of the communiqué, it was not a priority to the killer that the public read these words. Therefore, we can conclude that he was not trying to convince the public that he was in the park that night. Given these circumstances, the numerous antagonistic comments from Martin Lee, and the explicit introductory phrase, there is little doubt whom the killer was trying to convince, namely Martin Lee. This is interesting because it's not even clear if Lee believed his own rhetoric. The Chief of Inspectors was attempting to minimize public concern by painting the killer in an ineffectual light; the absolute accuracy of each of his statements was probably a lesser concern. If Lee secretly accepted the possibility that the killer was in the area, he certainly was not going to acknowledge it publicly.

So what are we to make of the killer's claim about the dogs and where he was? The first observation that strikes me is the use of the term "blocks" to describe his position relative to the dogs. He supposedly hid in a wooded area, yet he described his location in terms of city blocks. Why? While one could make other arguments, I suspect the reason he was thinking in terms of city blocks was because of his methodology. As evidenced by the way the killer knew Washington and Maple Streets, but he did not refer to Cherry Street by name, the killer's crime scenes were, first and foremost, points on a map and, therefore, that's how he understood them. He could visualize how the block boundaries extended into the wooded area because he had studied the location on his map of San Francisco. This is why he was comfortable using the word "blocks" when other people likely would have used different words to describe the distance and relationship.

Charlie Beene, the SFPD sergeant in charge of the night-shift dog unit, led the search for the fugitive on that October night in 1969.[*] In 2011, I had the opportunity to talk with Beene at length about the events of that evening. The first point that he clarified was the particular type of canine search that his dog unit performed. Specifically, the dogs did not do tracking, as people sometimes assume. Rather, they used scent to find people hiding in areas where nobody was supposed to be, usually because the area had been otherwise cleared out as was the case when he led the search of a section of the Presidio Army post on the night in question. Once a dog identified the presence of a human, he or she would alert the handler who would then engage the individual.

The specialized search unit — which included Beene, his German shepherd, Darius, and five other dogs and their handlers[†] — arrived on the scene approximately forty-five minutes to an hour after the fugitive disappeared into the Presidio. The dog handlers were not very optimistic about finding the man given that he had such a generous head start. Nevertheless, felony fugitive searches were the dog unit's specialty, and Beene was determined to conduct the most thorough search possible given the circumstances.

Beene's first order of business was to clear out everyone who had been occupying the area of interest. This included police officers on motorcycles and in patrol cars, some of whom had been riding around off road in various areas of the park, as well as other officers

---

[*]Charlie Beene went on to have a long and eventful career with the SFPD. He rose to the rank of captain of the Tactical Company, the organizational division that included all special units such as the dog unit, the bomb squad, and SWAT. Beene also wrote three books and implemented multiple creative policing programs, including a successful decoy unit.

[†]Martin Lee mentioned seven dogs; however, Beene recalled his team at the time included himself plus five other handlers.

on foot and a platoon of about thirty soldiers from the Presidio. For purposes of organization, Beene divided the search area into thirds. The SFPD officers on the scene were assigned to the western third; the platoon of soldiers was assigned to the eastern third; and Beene and the dog unit searched the center third — the area where the killer was most likely to be found, assuming he wasn't already long gone.

Combining Beene's description of the search and the killer's version of events — putting aside for the moment the question of whether or not we believe him — we can make a few observations. First, the killer's claim that the dogs were to the west places him in the eastern third of the search area, the section that soldiers from the Presidio were searching. Second, the statement that "the dogs never came within 2 blocks of me" sounds like a remarkably apt description of the search protocol because there was a definite eastern boundary that the dogs and their handlers did not cross, in other words, the division between the center third and the eastern third of the search area.

Taking into account that the killer addressed this passage to Martin Lee and not the public, the accurate description of the location of the dogs, the implied correctness of the unpublicized search protocol, and the detailed description of the motorcycle activity, there is a strong likelihood that the killer did, in fact, stay in the area, just as he said he did.

> *ps. 2 cops pulled a goof abot 3*
> *min after I left the cab. I was*
> *walking down the hill to the*
> *park when this cop car pulled up*
> *+ one of them called me over*
> *+ asked if I saw any one*
> *acting supicisous or strange*
> *in the last 5 to 10 min + I said*
> *yes there was this man who*
> *was runnig by waveing a gun*
> *+ the cops peeled rubber +*

> *Went around the corner as*
> *I directed them + I disap-*
> *eared into the park a block +*
> *a half away never to be seen*
> *again.*

Although the exact nature of the occurrence has been a subject of much debate among people who are knowledgeable about the case, the fact is that some type of encounter took place between the Zodiac and two SFPD officers in a patrol car — Officers Donald Fouke and Eric Zelms — as the killer walked east on Jackson Street before heading into the Presidio. Either the patrol car slowed and the officers simply observed the man, as Fouke claimed, or they stopped and conversed with the man, as the killer claimed.

> *Hey pig doesnt it rile you up*
> *To have your noze rubed in your*
> *booboos?*
> *If you cops think Im going to take*
> *on a bus the way I stated I was,*
> *you deserve to have holes in your*
> *heads.*

With this passage, the killer introduced the description of his first bus bomb. Essentially, he said he would not "take on" a bus in the way he described in the Stine Letter. Instead, he was going to target a school bus using an explosive device like the one he was about to describe.

> *What you do not know*
> *is whether the death machine*
> *is at the sight or whether*
> *it is being stored in my*
> *basement for future use.*

Much has been made about the killer's use of the term "basement" in this statement. Basements are quite rare in California, especially in the Bay Area. If taken at face value, this sentence clearly implies that the killer resided somewhere with a basement. Proponents of suspect Arthur Leigh Allen are often quick to point out that Allen lived in a house that did, in fact, have a basement. Be that as it may, I'm reluctant to assign much significance to this inference. There is no way to tell if the killer made this statement honestly, if he simply had previously lived in an area where basements were more common, or if he was intentionally being deceptive.

One intriguing possibility regarding the evolution of the bus bomb threat is that, in one of the *Chronicle*'s articles published in the wake of the Stine murder, Paul Avery may have inadvertently inspired the killer to consider using a bomb in pursuit of his terroristic goals.[25] The article of note included the following paragraph concerning school buses:

> *Even before starting on its routes each vehicle has undergone a thorough check to make sure a bomb isn't aboard. Someone hinting he might be Zodiac has telephoned such a threat in Santa Rosa.**

It's a near certainty that the real Zodiac was not responsible for the Santa Rosa threat; however, he likely read the article. Moreover, just three weeks later, he mailed a bomb threat of his own. His was more complicated, if not convoluted and impractical, but, nevertheless, its intended purpose was similar.

---

*San Francisco Chronicle. Newspaper index by Bell & Howell Co. Reproduced with permission of Newspaper Indexing Center, Micro Photo Division, B via Copyright Clearance Center.

2.7   The Belli Christmas Letter | December 20, 1969

Dear Melvin

The informality of this greeting is of interest. No "Mr. Belli" or "Sir," but rather "Melvin." Perhaps the Sam episode involving *A.M. San Francisco* discussed in Section 3.3 of *The Zodiac Revisited, Volume 1* served to convince the Zodiac that famed San Francisco attorney Melvin Belli really did have the killer's best interests at heart. Perhaps Sam, though clearly not the Zodiac, served as a surrogate for the killer and, in so doing, allowed the Zodiac to develop a perceived relationship with Belli.

> *I am finding it extreamly dif-*
> *icult to hold it in check I am*
> *afraid I will loose control*
> *again and take my nineth +*
> *possibly tenth victom.*

First, based on this statement, the implied victim count at this point was up to eight. In other words, the Zodiac wanted the public to believe that since writing his last letter five weeks earlier, he had murdered another person. Of course, this was almost certainly untrue. With this claim, the killer began the process of continuously increasing his victim count, a practice that served two purposes: (a) taunting the recipients (both direct and indirect) of his writing and (b) injecting elements of doubt and uncertainty into the circumstances of the case.

Second, the clear implication from the above sentence is that the Zodiac was in a precarious state of mental control and that previous victims had been murdered during periods that were characterized by this lack of control. This notion is the basis for the previously-described idea that the killer wrote the Belli Letter as a substitute for the act of killing. The Zodiac was describing how, at the moment, he was able to avoid the act of killing. Yet, with the passing of the winter solstice and the accompanying one-year anniversary of the Lake Herman Road murders, the killer felt compelled to act in some capacity; hence, the letter.

Whether or not the above statement was an accurate self-perception of the killer's mental and motivational state is a different question altogether. It may have been largely accurate, it may have simply been a convenient way to couch the content of the letter, or it may have been the killer hedging his bets by way of laying the groundwork for an insanity plea in the event that he was apprehended. As with so much of the story, we can say relatively little for certain. Nevertheless, there was likely at least a grain of truth to these remarks.

> *At*
> *the moment the children are*
> *safe from the bomb because*
> *it is so massive to dig in + the*
> *triger mech requires much work*
> *to get it adjusted just right.*

This description of the bomb stands in stark contrast to the description given by the killer just five weeks earlier when he wrote the following in the Bus Bomb Letter:

> *the system check out from*
> *one end to the other in my*
> *tests. What you do not know*
> *is whether the death machine*
> *is at the sight or whether*
> *it is being stored in my*
> *basement for future use.*

Now, with the later letter, apparently the system no longer checked out from end to end, and, moreover, the killer was implying that he had not deployed the alleged explosive device. Continuing from the Belli Letter:

> *But*
> *if I hold back too long from*
> *no nine I will loose* ~~*complet*~~ *all*
> *controol of my self + set the*
> *bomb up.*

A careful consideration of the correction that the writer made reveals a level of semantic sophistication that contradicts the Zodiac's apparent linguistic incompetence. Given this edit, it's clear that the killer was about to write "I will lose complete control" when he realized that the phrase did not convey his thought correctly. The notion that he wanted to communicate was "I will completely lose control," or alternatively "I will lose control completely." But what he was about to write was "I will lose complete control." This choice of words is not articulating the correct idea because one can lose "complete control" and yet maintain some degree of "partial control" or even a significant degree of partial control. Upon realizing this inaccuracy, the killer crossed out the partially written word and replaced it with "all," which conveyed a meaning equivalent to the original thought.

By striking through these seven letters and replacing the incomplete word with another, the killer allowed a true reflection of his intellect to escape the boundaries of his manufactured persona. This correction was not the product of somebody who was inexperienced with words. Nor was it done by somebody who was incompetent in the art of communication. Moreover, this fix certainly was not made by somebody who misspelled words like a poorly performing elementary school student. Rather, this correction was the work of an articulate wordsmith; one who was pretending to be something he was not.

2.8   The "My Name Is" Letter | April 20, 1970

After his letter to Melvin Belli, it would be another four months before the Zodiac spoke directly to the public. Following his standard introduction, the author opened the "My Name Is" Letter with the following question:

> *By the way have you cracked*
> *The last cipher I sent you?*

Of course, the killer was referring to the 340 cipher, which remained unsolved until December 2020. I suspect the killer honestly anticipated somebody would solve the cipher, perhaps not immediately, but eventually. In general, the author likely expected that the media, law enforcement, and the public would be able to decipher and interpret his communiqués in ways that have largely eluded everyone.

> *My name is –*
> A E N ⊕ ⊗ K ⊗ M ⊗ ⋏ N A M

By the height of the Zodiac hysteria following the murder of Paul Stine, city, county, and state government officials, not to mention the public, were desperate to identify the serial killer in their midst. The unusual nature of some of the approaches that were used illustrated the unconventional creativity involved. It also reflected the extreme lengths to which some people were willing to go in the off chance that the endeavor might prove successful. For example, Napa County Sheriff's Captainf Don Townsend promised to buy the killer "the best dinner in town" if he turned himself in.[26] The *Examiner* published open letters to the killer offering "... fair treatment, the assurance of medical help and the full benefits of your legal rights," as well as an opportunity for the killer to tell his story.[27,28] Subsequently, the newspaper got even more creative and encoded a message to the killer using the symbols from his first cryptogram.[29] California Attorney General Tom Lynch made a more direct appeal to the killer, simply asking that he turn himself in before "tragedy is written in blood."[18]

About the time of these quotes, on October 22, 1969, the *Examiner* published "a challenge perhaps unique in the annals of American crime...."[30] In an article entitled "Cipher Expert Dares Zodiac To 'Tell' Name," the president of the American Cryptogram Association, Dr. D. C. B. Marsh, issued the following challenge:

> *I invite 'Zodiac' to send ... a cipher code — however complicated — which will truly and honestly include his name — for study by myself and my colleagues in the association.*

Exactly six months after the publication of that challenge, both the *Examiner* and the *Chronicle* published news of the killer's latest letter, one that included a cipher prefaced by the phrase: "My name is — ."[31,32] Though the significance of the timing and the content seem to have gone unnoticed, there is little doubt that the killer's letter was a belated acceptance of Marsh's challenge.

> *I am mildly cerous as to how*
> *much money you have on my*
> *head now.*

Here we have another instance of the killer using a euphemism to minimize his self-portrayal of emotion, similar to the example from the Bus Bomb Letter, in which he described himself as "rather angry" when every other indication suggested that he was seething. In this case, instead of being "mildly" curious, it's much more likely that the killer was craving any and every detail he could get regarding law enforcement's perception of him. Yet, he downplayed his true emotions, perhaps as part of an effort to suggest a level of emotional detachment.

The idea of inquiring "how much money you have on my head" may have stemmed from the Yellow Cab Company's $1,000 reward "for information leading to the arrest and conviction of the person(s) responsible" for killing Charles Jarman (Section 4.4 of *The Zodiac*

Revisited, Volume 1), a murder many people initially attributed to the Zodiac.[33] As an interesting aside, SFPD Inspectors Armstrong and Toschi eventually collected the reward for solving Jarman's murder. Commendably, the two public servants donated the money to the murdered taxicab driver's wife.[34]

> *I hope you do not*
> *think that I was the one*
> *who wiped out that blue*
> *meannie[†] with a bomb at the*
> *cop station. Even though I talked*
> *about killing school children with*
> *one.*

The incident the killer described was the Park Station bombing, which was detailed in (Section 5.1 of *The Zodiac Revisited, Volume 1*). The perpetrator(s) detonated a pipe bomb outside the SFPD police station on Monday, February 16, 1970. The attack resulted in the death of officer Brian McDonnell and the injury of several others. In a move that provides some perspective to the Zodiac case, a coalition of community members posted a $35,000 reward in the hopes of flushing out the person or people responsible for the disturbing act of domestic terrorism. It didn't work. The bombing remains unsolved as of this book's publication.

It's difficult to overstate the extent of the shock and outrage that gripped the San Francisco community in the wake of the Park Station bombing. Ronald Reagan, who was governor of California at the time, likened the crime to the acts of guerrilla warfare occurring routinely in war-torn Vietnam. He asked the federal government to investigate the egregious criminal action. Meanwhile, state lawmakers scrambled to create legislation that would address the public's concerns in the aftermath of the explosion. The Bay Area in 1970 was

---

[†]As noted by many people before me, "blue meanie" was a then-common slang term for a police officer popularized by the 1968 Beatles movie *Yellow Submarine*.

a tumultuous environment in which violence and murder were relatively commonplace; however, this criminal act seemed to cross a line and offend the sensibilities of nearly everyone.

Perhaps it was just a coincidence, or perhaps it was thinly veiled narcissism, but the *Examiner* detailed the Park Station bombing in an article published over a month after the tragedy.[35] That story was immediately below an article about the Zodiac: "Rode With Zodiac, Woman Claims."[36] The subject matter, of course, was Kathleen Johns's ordeal. Hence, through the price-on-my-head comment and the mention of the Park Station bombing, the killer managed to indirectly reference the only two substantive Zodiac articles that San Francisco newspapers had published since the fervor over the Belli Letter had dissipated.

> *It just wouldnt doo to*
> *move in on someone elses teritory.*

Subscribers to the Taking Credit theory are often quick to dismiss instances where a consistent application of the theory predicts action, yet none occurred. Whether it be the San Jose murders of Deborah Furlong and Kathy Snoozy (which took law enforcement nearly two years to solve and, at one point, the media had all but attributed to the Zodiac), the murder of taxicab driver Charles Jarman in Presidio Heights (again, which the media speculated the Zodiac had perpetrated), or the bombing death of Sergeant McDonnell, additional opportunities for deceitful claims of responsibility were never far. Yet, unlike the reference to his "Riverside activity," the killer never wrote and gave police credit for stumbling across any "San Jose activity." And despite the fact that nobody seemed to be seriously suggesting that the Zodiac was responsible for McDonnell's death, the killer went out of his way to deny involvement. Moreover, two of the three crimes that the killer opted not to take credit for went on to be solved — the Park Station bombing and the resulting murder of Officer McDonnell remain unsolved. In contrast, all the crimes for which the killer either took credit or is suspected of committing — partially based on self-implication — have remained unsolved.

> *But there is more glory in killing*
> *a cop than a cid because a cop*
> *can shoot back.*

This twisted assessment of Sergeant McDonnell's death seemed to foreshadow the ambush of SFPD Officer Richard Radetich, who was killed two months after this letter was written.

> *I have killed*
> *Ten people to date.*
> *It would have been a lot more except*
> *That my bus bomb was a dud.*
> *I was swamped out by the*
> *Rain we had a while back.*

In Section 5.2.5.1 of *The Zodiac Revisited, Volume 2*, I offered a probable solution for the 32 cipher, which was supposed to identify the location of the killer's bus bomb. The location I proposed corresponds to a site somewhere along Stevens Canyon Road in the city of Cupertino. In 1970, a weekly newspaper named the *Cupertino Courier* served the area.

We know that the time frame for the "rain we had a while back" comment referred to sometime between the Belli Letter from December 20, 1969, and this letter, which was postmarked April 20, 1970 — with the expectation that the time in question would not be too recent given the use of the phrase "a while back." Sifting through the *Cupertino Courier* between the dates in question and looking for reports of excessive rain does yield some results. In particular, the paper published an article titled "It was a Very Wet Week Here" on January 14, 1970.[37] In it, the author documented the most recent storm, which dumped 2.17 inches of rain, as well as some of the chaos that resulted from a driver losing control of his vehicle and hitting a power pole due to slippery road conditions. A follow-up story a week later reported on more excessive rain, flood conditions in some parts of the county, and additional power outages.[38]

Of course, discovering that it rained during California's rainy season is not surprising in and of itself. But these two articles are more meaningful than that. My proposed solution to the 32 cipher identified a specific geographic location. The killer wrote about the supposed location, mentioning that it was "swamped out" a "while back" in a way that suggested local people would have recognized the description. And finally, the local newspaper that served the area in question explicitly documented excessive rain and related flooding for one time — and one time only — in the correct part of the expected time frame. While not definitive, these circumstances are compelling.

As discussed when proposing the solution to the 32 cipher, the fact that the killer had chosen a specific location that he described through the combination of the cipher and the map does not necessarily mean he built and deployed the explosive device. He may have done neither, he may have done both, or he may have experimented with building the device but never actually deployed it. All we know for certain is that no such device was ever found.

2.9   Dragon Card | April 28, 1970

Just over a week after receiving the "My Name Is" Letter and cipher from the Zodiac, the *Chronicle* received what has come to be known as the Dragon Card (see Section 5.4 of *The Zodiac Revisited, Volume 1*). The inside of the card read:

> *Sorry to hear your ass is a dragon*

It's interesting to note that the cards the killer chose were always intended to be funny. The killer seemed to consider himself a jokester. Perhaps he was trying to communicate the idea, either consciously or subconsciously, that he found it humorous that law enforcement seemed unable to capture him. Or perhaps he viewed himself as laughing at the police — much like the description of Dr. Zodiac from *Charlie Chan at Treasure Island* (see Section 4.1.2 of *The Zodiac Revisited, Volume 2*) — and he was sarcastically inviting them to laugh along with him. For this particular card, he likely viewed the joke "your ass is a dragon" to be apropos of the situation given that the police were not moving fast enough to catch him. One thing is certain, whatever entertainment value the killer derived from the card was not shared by anyone on the receiving end of the communiqué.

> *I hope you enjoy your selves*
> *when I have my Blast.*

In the above taunting sentiment, the killer could have simply said something like: "Soon I'll have my Blast." But this wasn't satisfactory. He wanted to indicate not only that he would be having his "Blast" but also that he hoped others would derive pleasure from the activity. Of course, the idea is ridiculous; if he would've had his so-called blast, he would've been the only person to enjoy it.

> *If you dont want me to*
> *have this blast you must*
> *do two things. 1 Tell every*
> *one about the bus bomb with*
> *all the details.*

To be honest, it's a bit surprising that the killer didn't make some kind of threat like this one sooner. By the time the killer sent the Dragon Card, six months had passed since he wrote the Bus Bomb Letter. However, at the behest of the SFPD, the *Chronicle* had not reported on it. It may be that the killer was not entirely happy with the shortcomings of the original bus bomb diagram, as evidenced by his acknowledgment of some difficulty with the triggering mechanism in his letter to Melvin Belli. In this sense, he may have actually been OK with the paper not acknowledging his threat. In fact, many aspects of the Bus Bomb Letter suggest that it was written hastily in a fit of anger. Perhaps he regretted making the initial bomb threat prematurely. In any event, he finally did make an updated bomb threat with his new and improved explosive contraption. Whatever the reason he had for his previous tolerance, it was now gone. Just eight days after the killer mailed his updated bomb threat to the *Chronicle*, he followed up with this card, making it clear that continuing to suppress his threat was unacceptable.

> *... 2 I would like*
> *to see some nice Zodiac buttons*
> *wandering about town. Every*
> *one else has these buttons like,*
> *⊕, black power, melvin eats*
> *bluber, etc. Well it would cheer*
> *me up considerably if I saw*
> *a lot of people wearing my*
> *buton. Please no nasty ones*
> *like melvin's*

There are a few themes running through the Zodiac communications where it's genuinely difficult to figure out what to make of them. The idea that the man believed he was collecting slaves for his afterlife is an example of one such theme. Did he really believe what he claimed? Was it a contrived basis for an insanity plea in the event of his apprehension? Or was it something else? Another example is this idea of expecting the Bay Area public to wear buttons designed to communicate a connection with, if not support for, an unapprehended serial killer in their midst. My sense, after taking into consideration all of his writing and other known actions, is that he was sincere in this request. Whether or not he truly thought it would happen is a different question; one whose answer is less clear.

Claiming that seeing the buttons would "cheer me up considerably" is a noteworthy self-characterization of the man's mental state. His letter to Melvin Belli conveyed vivid imagery where he seemed to honestly describe certain aspects of his mental disorder. Here in the Dragon Card, he practically implied that he was suffering from depression. One has to wonder if the killer understood that he was in the grips of a mental disorder. These two communiqués suggest that he was aware, at least on some level.

The whole button theme is reminiscent of the Dripping Pen Card from the previous November where he claimed that if the newspaper did not publish news of him, he would get so lonely he would "do his thing." In that context, it was the citizens of the Bay Area reading about him that provided the man with some sense of connectedness that clearly was otherwise lacking in his life. Six months later, he was looking for new and better ways to experience anonymous connection to his fellow members of society, as if publication in the newspaper was no longer providing an adequate fix. Of course, the irony here is that, if the man did not find evidence of people providing the connectedness that he so desperately longed to have, he was threatening to kill the very same people with whom he wanted to bond. This is the kind of logic that only makes sense to a disturbed mind.

The "melvin eats bluber" reference is an often-discussed curiosity. The type of buttons to which the Zodiac was referring were commonly worn counterculture accessories. One particular manufacturer created what turned out to be a surprisingly popular button that read "Shakespeare Eats Bacon." This phrase, which also occasionally showed up in graffiti, was a bit of an inside joke for literature types who were familiar with the well-known but little-accepted theory that Sir Francis Bacon actually wrote the works that are attributed to William Shakespeare. As a follow-up to that button, the same manufacturer created one using the phrase "Herman Melville Eats Blubber," which was a less meaningful reference to the author of the classic whaling novel *Moby Dick*.

The consensus among people who have thought about the subject seems to be that the Zodiac purposely dropped "Herman" and substituted "Melville" with "Melvin" to create an insult directed at Melvin Belli. This does seem to be the most likely explanation.

Assuming the killer did craft the example as an insult to Belli, one has to wonder what triggered his newfound hostility toward the famed Bay Area attorney. Just four months earlier, the killer's personalized Christmas letter to Belli had demonstrated a very cordial and friendly tone. I suspect the answer to this question has to do with how Belli handled the Zodiac's interest in communicating with him. As mentioned in Section 4.3 of *The Zodiac Revisited, Volume 1*, Melvin Belli was away on business in Europe at the time the killer's letter arrived. Furthermore, an FBI memo documented someone claiming to be the killer calling Belli's residence and talking to the housekeeper during the same time frame. Some other stories claim the killer visited Belli's residence and talked to the housekeeper, although these stories are not as well-documented. Relatedly, Zodiac researcher Ricardo Eugirtni Gomez has a compelling theory that the killer stylized the numbers of the address on the envelope of the Belli Letter, shown in Figure 2.1, to precisely match the physical display of the address at Belli's residence.[39] Taken together these circumstances paint a picture of somebody who was especially interested in meeting with Belli.

It seems that the killer just had bad timing. During Christmas-time 1969, Belli was in Europe for several weeks. The attorney said he would drop everything and fly back to meet with the killer, but the Zodiac would have to reach out and request the meeting explicitly. Then, on December 30, the *Chronicle* published an article that may well have rubbed the killer the wrong way. In it, Belli instructed the Zodiac to communicate with him via the *Chronicle*.[40] In other words, the killer should telephone or write the newspaper and a representative of the paper would pass the information along, supposedly in confidence, to Belli. Given that the killer had written Belli personally, phoned his residence, and possibly even visited the lawyer's home, the killer may have interpreted Belli's instruction to funnel communication through the *Chronicle* as a slight, a step backward that diminished the value of what the killer perceived to be an existing relationship.

Figure 2.1: The envelope from the Belli Letter with its uniquely stylized numbering, likely crafted to match the address displayed outside of Melvin Belli's San Francisco residence. Image reproduced with permission from the *San Francisco Chronicle* / Polaris.

Of course, we are left to evaluate the case of the Zodiac based on the reality that was. There are, however, a handful of small details that, had they played out differently, may well have had a substantial impact on events. The most notable example occurred in the immediate aftermath of the Stine murder. If the SFPD had broadcast the correct description of the suspect — a white male, not a black male — the killer's encounter with law enforcement on Jackson Street undoubtedly would have unfolded much differently. Similarly, if Belli had stayed in San Francisco during the Christmas season of 1969, there is a strong probability he would have had a meaningful interaction with the killer that, conceivably, could have led to his surrender.

2.10 The Button Letter | June 26, 1970

The Zodiac next communicated just under two months later when he sent the meaningful and important Button Letter.

> *I have become very upset with*
> *the people of San Fran Bay*
> *Area. They have not complied*
> *with my wishes for them to*
> *wear some nice ⊕ buttons.*

It's interesting to note that the literary monotone present in earlier letters was gone at this point — although it would return in the very next letter. Uncharacteristically, the killer just came out and said that he was "very upset." Also, these first two sentences did not include the normal grammatical and spelling errors that had come to characterize the killer's writing. Perhaps the author started writing before consciously embracing the techniques that he normally used to hide aspects of his true self.

While there probably is an element of truth to the connectedness theme in the killer's request that people wear ⊕ buttons, it's difficult to evaluate to what degree the dialogue was otherwise sincere, and, therefore, it's hard to take some of his continued ramblings too seriously. Did he really expect people to start wearing such buttons? It's doubtful. Instead, this line of discussion was probably just a device to couch some of his communication.

> *I promised to punish them*
> *if they did not comply, by*
> *anilating a full School Buss.*

At this point, the spelling errors came back with a vengeance. The idea that the killer had no problem spelling the word "complied" but then stumbled on "bus" feels improbable, especially given that he'd managed to spell "bus" correctly on multiple occasions previously.

This is more evidence that the author's ostensible spelling problems were really just part of a larger effort to misrepresent his true cognitive abilities. Moreover, it appears that one of the ways in which the killer created fake spelling errors was by incorrectly doubling up consonants, as in "buss" and "figgure."

I shot a man sitting in
a parked car with a .38.

Of course, this passage from the letter appears to be a reference to the murder of Officer Richard Radetich, which is discussed in Section 5.5 of *The Zodiac Revisited, Volume 1* and later in Section 3.9.

⊕–12   *SFPD–0*

The killer had not mentioned his supposed murder count since the "My Name Is" Letter back in April. At that time, the alleged count was ten. Now, just two months later, he was claiming he'd killed twelve. Of course, struggling to make sense of the killer's score is almost certainly an exercise in futility, as is clearly evidenced in this letter. The ongoing score was simply a device the killer used to increase the level of ambiguity and, in turn, heighten the terroristic impact of his crimes.

Nevertheless, this letter is important because, for the first time, the murder score had evolved into its final form. The Dripping Pen Card had a victim count that included the alleged months of activity. In the Bus Bomb Letter, the killer included the *X*'ed Zodiac symbol, which was a cryptic summary of his crimes. The Belli Letter had an implied murder count. The "My Name Is" Letter had the first explicit declaration of a murder count. And finally, with the Button Letter, the killer settled on the succinct version of his taunting device in which he wrote a murder count associated with himself and assigned a value of zero to the SFPD.

Where the Zodiac came up with the idea of taunting his readers by way of an ongoing, ever-increasing score is unknown. But research into the San Francisco newspaper articles documenting the events of the Zodiac — articles the killer almost certainly read — yielded a curiosity.

On October 4, 1969, a week after the Lake Berryessa attack and a week before the Stine murder, the *Examiner* published a small article on page 3 noting that the Napa County Sheriff's Office was assigning four additional people to work on the case full-time.[41] To fill up some empty space on this page following the article, the *Examiner* inserted an advertisement promoting a sports-score service. Readers were given a local telephone number that they could use to receive recent sports scores, presumably through a recording. What's even more interesting than the nature of the advertisement is its attention-grabbing headline: "What's the Score?" (See Figure 2.2.) It's a minor stretch of the imagination to envision the killer reading this headline and saying to himself: "What's the score, indeed."

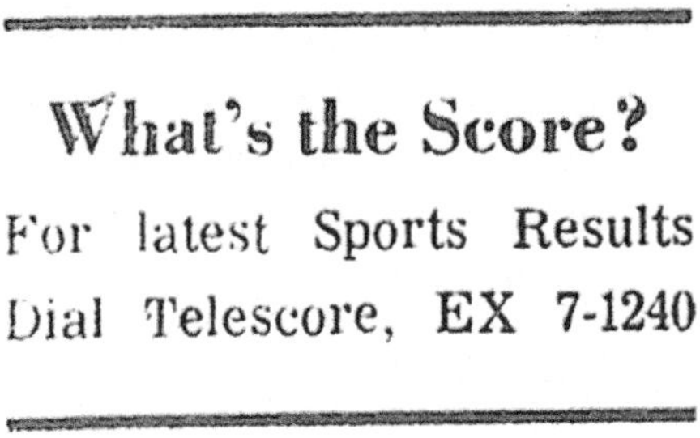

What's the Score?

For latest Sports Results
Dial Telescore, EX 7-1240

Figure 2.2: The advertisement at the end of the October 4, 1969, article published in the *San Francisco Examiner*

> *The Map coupled with this code will tell you where the bomb is set. You have untill next Fall to dig it up.* ⊕

As you may recall, the Zodiac included the 32 cipher in the Button Letter, and it was accompanied by a cutout map of the San Francisco Bay Area, which the killer had taken from the 1969

Phillips 66 map of California. Supposedly, these two components formed a puzzle that, once solved, would reveal the location where the killer was planning to plant his bus bomb. Regardless of whether or not he actually intended to follow through, it's a near certainty that the Zodiac invested a significant amount of time and effort into this challenge. Between delivering the map, the cipher, and the thinly veiled claim of responsibility for the murder of Officer Radetich, there is little doubt that the killer felt an exceptionally high level of perverse excitement regarding this letter.

2.11   The Kathleen Johns Letter | July 24, 1970

> *I am rather unhappy because*
> *you people will not wear some*
> *nice ⊕ buttons.*

By this point, it had been three months since the killer's initial request for people to start wearing "some nice Zodiac butons [*sic*]" and one month since his admonishment — and alleged punishment — of Bay Area residents for their noncompliance. Interestingly, his previous letter did not appear to renew his request for people to wear the buttons; it simply stated that people had not complied, and, therefore, the author had punished them. Apparently, despite having administered the supposed punishment, the demand still stood.

The phrase "rather unhappy" is more of the killer's deceptive nonemotional tone, his literary monotone. If we take the demand that people wear Zodiac buttons at face value, the killer was more likely livid than unhappy. In fact, the word "rather" appears to be an indicator for this practice of downplaying his honest emotions. As a general rule, if we replaced "rather" with "extremely," I believe we would have a more accurate representation of the killer's true emotional state.

> *So I now*
> *have a little list...*

The "little list" is obviously a precursor to the *Mikado* Letter that would follow two days later. Indeed, one has to wonder if perhaps the author had begun work on his five-page masterpiece by the time that he sent this short note.

> *... starting with*
> *the woeman + her baby that I*
> *gave a rather intersting ride*
> *for a coupple howers one*
> *evening a few months back that*
> *ended in my burning her*
> *car where I found them.*

For the second time in this short letter, the killer employed the telltale adverb "rather." The usage was effectively the same as the previous occurrence, in other words, more literary monotone.

There is no doubt that this passage was a reference to the Kathleen Johns incident; it was too precise to be anything else. However, we know the killer did not find Kathleen and her daughter in the manner implied in the letter. He followed Kathleen and convinced her to pull over by flashing his lights and honking his horn. Of course, we only know this because Kathleen lived to tell her story. These facts suggest that this curious choice of words may be a latent indication of the way the killer had intended his crime to be perceived. In other words, if the killer had successfully abducted and murdered a lone woman on that March evening, no one would have been wise to the ruse that he employed. From the evidence, it would have been a reasonable interpretation of the scene to conclude that the abductor happened upon the victim who, through no involvement of the killer, was having automotive problems.

2.12 The *Mikado* Letter | July 26, 1970

Between the Button Letter — with the 32 cipher and the Phillips 66 map — and the *Mikado* Letter, just one month later — containing the killer's one and only explicit clue and his extensive homage to "I've Got a Little List" — the summer of 1970 was a prolific, strange, and interesting time in terms of Zodiac letter writing.

Multiple elements of the *Mikado* Letter, including the near verbatim quoting of the "I've Got a Little List" libretto, are discussed at length in Section 4.1.3 of *The Zodiac Revisited, Volume 2.* I address the remainder of the content here.

> *Being that you will not wear*
> *some nice ⊕ buttons, how about*
> *wearing some nasty ⊕ buttons.*
> *Or any type of ⊕ buttons that*
> *you can think up.*

This opening request from the killer was uncharacteristic, almost desperate. The pleading was far removed from the demanding and pompous tone that we'd expect from him. It is, however, not entirely without parallel in that the change in tone was reminiscent of the "Could you print this new cipher on your front page?" postscript from the Dripping Pen Card. Perhaps unsurprisingly, these instances of generally uncharacteristic tone suggest that the killer's volatile mental state may have been prone to fluctuations. As was also evidenced in the Belli Letter, this mental instability likely played a role in thwarting a behavioral consistency that we might otherwise have expected to see — for example, demonstrating a stricter adherence to methodology.

> *If you do*
> *not wear any type of ⊕*
> *buttons I shall (on top of every*
> *thing else) torture all 13*
> *of my slaves that I have*
> *wateing for me in Paradice.*

Again, as was the case with the Dripping Pen Card, the killer's deviation from his more typical attitude was exceptionally short-lived.

This introductory threat and the torture-based fantasy montage that follows both reinforced an aspect of the killer's psyche that we've come to understand: he was motivated by a sadistic pleasure that he experienced through the infliction of both emotional and physical pain onto others. In all likelihood, the afterlife fantasy was simply a device to establish an insanity plea. Nonetheless, the psychological gratification the killer experienced through the shared communication of these torture fantasies was very much real.

Honestly, the specifics of the torture-fantasy prose are unimportant; they offer little in terms of furthering our overall understanding. Generally, it's the larger torture-based motif that deserves our attention. Of course, the one exception to this assertion is the line:

> *Some I shall tie over ant hills*
> *and watch them scream + twich*
> *and squirm.*

As detailed in Section 1.2.2, this sentence provided very compelling evidence that the Zodiac and the murderer of Cheri Jo Bates were one and the same.

2.13   The Crackproof Card | October 6, 1970

With the *Mikado* Letter arriving during the *Chronicle*'s self-imposed abstention from reporting on Zodiac communiqués, there was little news about the killer in the months following the Button Letter. The newspaper abandoned its commitment to Zodiac silence with the arrival of the Crackproof Card, reporting on both it and the *Mikado* Letter simultaneously.

As we've seen in our consideration of the killer's use of circles instead of dots, he had a penchant for consciously introducing idiosyncrasies into his communications that further established his identity. In the case of his pasted-up cards—this card being one and the Peek Through the Pines Card being the other—there are two such idiosyncrasies on display: (a) the use of a hole punch—this card included thirteen holes punched along one side, which clearly represented the thirteen victims the killer was claiming to have murdered — and (b) the inclusion of upside-down text.

Because the Crackproof Card was the first of the two pasted-up communiqués, these idiosyncrasies would have just seemed odd when the card arrived. They didn't represent a repeated pattern until the arrival of the Peek Through the Pines Card.

*'Some of Them Fought
It Was Horrible'*

This statement is yet another indication of the psychological pleasure that the killer got from his sadistic fantasies. He enjoyed the idea of his victims suffering. He undoubtedly enjoyed reliving the physical and emotional pain he inflicted upon his past victims. He likely included this sentence because he found it gratifying to imagine the reader horrified at the thought of his sadistic actions.

Fk I'm crackproof.

Conventional wisdom is that "Fk" is short for "Fuck". Although we cannot say for sure, this interpretation is likely correct. In all his writing, the killer used relatively little profanity. The two notable exceptions included this quote from the Debut of the Zodiac Letter:

Bullshit that area is surrounded by high hills and trees.

and this description from the Bus Bomb Letter:

... set the shit off ...

While these examples demonstrate a basic willingness of the killer to use profanity, it's also true that society judges the word "fuck" to be considerably worse than the word "shit" (in all its various forms). These circumstances suggest the killer was simply not comfortable writing — or in this particular case, constructing out of newspaper clippings — the word "fuck." Indeed, another example from the letter of August 2, 1969, in which the killer first referred to himself as the Zodiac, gives credence to this hypothesis. When describing how the pay phone he had just hung up started to ring, the killer censored himself by writing: " ... the damn X@ thing began to ring...." More than likely, the word he was self-censoring was "fucking," especially since he had already written the word "bullshit" in the same letter.

This desire to communicate the word "fuck" combined with a simultaneous unwillingness to write it hints at a certain degree of emotional immaturity, possibly rooted in the killer's relationship with authority. The man was willing to murder innocent people in cold blood, yet he was afraid to violate a social norm that prohibited the use of the word "fuck." If nothing else, these circumstances suggest the killer was raised in an environment where the use of such profanity was frowned upon, and, furthermore, he likely didn't use it on a regular basis in his adult life.

Apart from the question of the ambiguous letters "Fk," this sentence is also the most valuable on the card because of the word "crackproof." The authenticated *Los Angeles Times* Letter, which would be written five months later, also used this word. If we are to believe that the Zodiac didn't send the Crackproof Card, then somebody pretending to be the killer sent it to the *Chronicle*, and the Zodiac, after reading about the fake communiqué, reacted by using its unique terminology in a letter he wrote less than six months later. This scenario is unlikely.

What is the price tag now?

The "price tag" undoubtedly referred to the reward offered for information leading to the arrest of the killer. This line of questioning was a continuation of the theme first established in the "My Name Is" Letter, in which the Zodiac asked " ... how much money you have on my head now." Clearly, the killer was experiencing a significant sense of satisfaction knowing that he was an exceptionally wanted man.

2.14   The Halloween Card | October 27, 1970

Just three weeks later, the Zodiac mailed a Halloween card to *Chronicle* reporter Paul Avery — notably misspelling his last name as "Averly." In so doing, he provided the case evidence with one of its most intriguing communiqués.

The general consensus was that the comment "You Are Doomed" represented a death threat against Avery. San Francisco homicide detectives William Armstrong and David Toschi both agreed that there was no question regarding the interpretation. The two theorized that, as the principal author of the *Chronicle*'s Zodiac stories, some aspect of Avery's reporting had piqued the ire of the killer. The reporter concurred, stating:

> *"It just looks like Zodiac has gotten sore at some of the things I have written about him," Avery said. "He is unquestionably a shrewd individual and has, quite correctly, read between the lines and knows I disbelieve his ever-mounting claims as to the number of persons he says he has killed. I consider the 'you are doomed' to be more of the same — a lot of talk," Avery said.*[42]

But was the comment really a death threat directed at Avery? Perhaps. Another possibility, however, is that the killer was more abstractly directing the comment at his victims — both actual and alleged. In considering this possibility, it's instructive to note that dictionary.com defines the word as: to destine, especially to an adverse state.[43] Since the killer's fantasy world was premised upon the idea of his victims becoming his slaves in the afterlife, one reasonable interpretation is that all the Zodiac's victims were doomed.

It's difficult to imagine that the Zodiac honestly would have desired to harm Paul Avery because an overarching need for attention was the hallmark of the killer's behavior. And most of the attention he received came in the form of newspaper coverage, the majority of which was in the *Chronicle*, and most of it written by Paul Avery. The Zodiac likely viewed Avery not as a problem that needed to be eliminated but rather a valuable collaborator of sorts. Furthermore, it was probably this sentiment that motivated the Zodiac to single out Avery for special attention on Halloween 1970 not a desire to kill him.

Whether the "You Are Doomed" comment was an ill-conceived death threat or a misunderstood abstraction, its interpretation as a death threat would overshadow all other aspects of the Halloween communiqué, arguably to the detriment of the case.

As we have seen from analyzing the killer's methodology, the spatial information of the Halloween Card is one of the most valuable clues in the entirety of the evidence. The Zodiac likely sent this clue directly to Avery in the hopes that the reporter would be able to correctly interpret its meaning since he was one of the people most familiar with the details of the case. And then Avery could communicate his interpretation to the *Chronicle*'s readers. Unfortunately, the killer once again overestimated the extent to which people could reasonably infer information from vague clues such as those on the card. Instead of discerning elements of the killer's methodology, Avery obtained a permit to carry a concealed weapon.

Nevertheless, from the killer's perspective the endeavor was not a total loss. The public reaction to the Halloween Card included the response that soon led Avery to the so-called Riverside connection. So, while the Zodiac undoubtedly was hoping for newspaper coverage of one particular sort, he was likely satisfied with basking in the attention provided by coverage of a different sort. In all probability, it was the end rather than the means that truly mattered to him.

2.15   The *Los Angeles Times* Letter | March 13, 1971

Despite the significant coverage of the Zodiac's possible connection to the 1966 murder of Cheri Jo Bates in Riverside, California, the killer chose to abstain from further communication. Of particular note, there were no communiqués around the time of the winter solstice. Finally, in March 1970, the killer broke his silence by writing to the *Los Angeles Times*. This letter is important because it's the only authenticated instance of the Zodiac writing to a newspaper outside the Bay Area. Mailed from the city of Pleasanton, it preceded the Peek Through the Pines Card — which had a nearly perfect alignment with the spring equinox — by just nine days. Likely, the killer intended the news of the *Los Angeles Times* Letter to roughly correspond with the equinox, yet he opted to send it early in order to compensate for two potential issues. The first concern was simply the geographic distance between the Bay Area and Los Angeles. With the increased distance, the arrival time of the letter became less predictable. Apart from allowing the letter additional time to arrive, the killer further dealt with this complexity by marking the letter as "Air Mail" and affixing sufficient postage to cover the applicable domestic airmail rate.

The second uncertainty was the *Los Angeles Times* itself. Would the editorial staff sit on the letter while they decided whether or not to publish it? Would they consult with the *Chronicle*? Would they have it authenticated by the California Department of Justice? By this point in time, the process of writing to the *Chronicle* was a well-defined and predictable transaction — assuming they did not suppress the correspondence, as they had done with two of the killer's letters in the summer of 1970. The *Times*, on the other hand, was a completely different entity, undoubtedly sure to have variables all of its own. Furthermore, with less of a vested interest in a serial killer that was primarily operating in a city nearly 400 miles to the north, the question of how the *Times* would react was anything but certain. The killer likely concluded that the best way to deal with these unknown variables was, simply, to allow for some additional time.

As it turns out, the postal service's delivery was quick and the *Times*, although clearly thoughtful in its response, moved expeditiously. The newspaper arranged for John J. Harris, the former president of the American Society of Questioned Document Examiners, to compare the letter against other known writings of the Zodiac. He confirmed its authenticity and the *Times* published an article regarding the letter just three days after it had been postmarked.[44]

> *Like I have allways said*
> *I am crack proof.*

As discussed in Section 2.13, this comment provided compelling evidence that the Crackproof Card was indeed authentic.

> *I do have to give them*
> *credit for stumbling across*
> *my riverside activity, ...*

The phrase "stumbling across" paints the picture of law enforcement succeeding in spite of themselves. This backhanded compliment was the predictable style of the Zodiac that readers had come to expect based on his literary body of work to this point. The dual edges of this statement were clearly designed to take a jab at the police while, at the same time, allowing the author to bask in the infamy of taking responsibility for the death of Cheri Jo Bates. The characterization of the murder as his "Riverside activity" was more of the killer's literary monotone that would pass for a dry sense of humor were it not for the tragedy of the circumstances.

> *...but*
> *they are only finding the*
> *easy ones, there are a hell*
> *of a lot more down there.*

How many more is "a hell of a lot" when the subject is murder? I could reasonably argue that a single additional murder rightfully constitutes a hell of a lot more. Nevertheless, as described in Section 1.4, I believe this claim referred to four other people, namely: Robert Domingos and Linda Edwards, who were murdered in Gaviota on June 4, 1963, and Joyce and Johnny Ray Swindle, who were gunned down in San Diego on February 5, 1964.

The author of the *Times* story that documented the arrival of the Zodiac letter followed up with Riverside law enforcement regarding this claim. Police Captain Irvin Cross pointed out that his department had "no other unsolved murders." Captain Bud Brooks from the Riverside County Sheriff's Department commented that he had one open murder investigation that could be within the realm of possibility, although he discounted the likelihood of the killer being involved due to differences in modus operandi. Otherwise, he commented "I can't imagine what other cases he might be referring to."[44] The press and law enforcement were unable to see the forest for the trees.

> The reason that Im writing
> to the Times is this. They
> don't bury me on the back pages
> like some of the others.

In what some would call a coincidence and others a case of cause and effect, the *Times* ran a UPI story about the Zodiac on the front page exactly one week before the killer's letter to the paper was postmarked. This point is noteworthy because the newspaper published the article at a time when Zodiac stories were few and far between. The article reported the discovery of Lynda Kanes's body; she was a Pacific Union College student who had been missing. Because her shallow grave was discovered near Lake Berryessa, some had speculated that the Zodiac might have been responsible for her death. Regardless of whether or not this story provoked the killer to write to the *Times*, it's clear evidence that the newspaper did have an attitude toward covering the elusive fugitive that he would have appreciated.

Ironically, the *Chronicle* covered the arrival of the Zodiac's letter at the *Times* with a front-page blurb, whereas the *Times* itself relegated coverage to page 3.[44,45] The editorial staff at the *Times* almost certainly made this decision to deny the Zodiac the one thing he longed to have most: front-page coverage. This explanation is the only viable one that fits given the dynamics of the situation. Specifically, a week earlier, the Zodiac was featured on the front page of the newspaper by way of a UPI story that only included speculation about the Zodiac being involved in a Northern California murder. But when the killer wrote directly to the *Times* and took credit for an open homicide in Southern California, the story ended up on page 3. Clearly, the *Times* was uncomfortable acquiescing to the desires of a serial murderer.

Many people believe or assume that this statement regarding the killer's preference for the *Times* was based on prominent coverage that he had received during his reign of terror in the Bay Area. However, for the killer to have been monitoring the paper while living in the Bay Area would have been unlikely from a logistical standpoint. Moreover, it's important to point out that two out of the three Southern California attacks generated several front-page stories in the *Times*,[46-49] while the remaining murder, that of Cheri Jo Bates, was reported prominently on page 3.[4] Hence, the author would have had good reason to be happy with the coverage he received in the *Times* long before he even conceived of his Northern California persona.

SFPD–0   ⊕–17+

The obvious interpretation of the "17+" designation is that it should be broken down into two parts. Under this reading, the "17" referred to the number of victims the killer claimed to have accumulated as the Zodiac. Of course, this value was undoubtedly inflated but nonetheless consistent with the author's ongoing ploy.

The second part, the "+," represented an indeterminate number of victims the killer was acknowledging that he murdered before assuming the persona of the Zodiac. This explanation fits the context of the letter given that the missive contained the first and only claim of responsibility for a victim that fell outside the window of activity associated with the Zodiac. Furthermore, the "hell of a lot more" statement emphasized the unknown aspect of this quantity, which was succinctly represented by the "+."

After going public with some of my thoughts regarding the Zodiac's likely use of the compass rose as an element of his methodology, Zodiac researcher Mike Rodelli suggested to me that the "17+" could be interpreted as having a duality whereby it also represented magnetic north in the Bay Area, in other words, 17° east. In this case the "+" would indicate a clockwise rotation since that is the positive direction of angular measure. This observation is interesting and certainly a distinct possibility, especially given that the score was clearly inflated, and, therefore, the killer could have easily chosen a value that coincided with some other meaningful aspect of his activity.

2.16 The Peek Through the Pines Card
March 22, 1971

On Monday, March 22, less than two weeks after the *Los Angeles Times* received its letter from the Zodiac, an observant postal inspector noticed the Peek Through the Pines Card and recognized it as a likely communiqué from the serial killer. The spring equinox that year occurred the day before. While we cannot say for certain when the killer dropped the card in the mail, its discovery correlated exceptionally well with the equinox. Unlike the *Times* missive, the killer knew exactly how to manage the timing of this correspondence.

With the arrival of this card, a connection was evident between it and the Crackproof Card — namely the use of a hole punch and the upside-down text. And with the Crackproof Card's connection to the authenticated *Los Angeles Times* Letter by way of the killer's use of the word "crackproof," we can begin to appreciate a consistency running through all three of these communications.

Additionally, the Peek Through the Pines Card has another such oddity in that the killer misspelled Paul Avery's last name as "Averly," exactly as he'd done on the envelope containing the Halloween Card that was sent directly to Avery. Make no mistake about it, as described earlier, Paul Avery was an important man to the Zodiac, and the killer knew how to spell his last name. This misspelling and that of the Halloween Card are simply additional instances of consciously created idiosyncrasies intended to strengthen — but not incontrovertibly establish — the killer's identity.

Finally, Sherwood Morrill's assessment of what little handwriting was present on the Peek Through the Pines Card reinforced the idea that this communiqué was authentic.

Sought victim 12

If we carefully consider the ever-increasing victim count, as enumerated in Table 2.1, it quickly becomes evident that there is a problem with the killer's claim noted above, especially if we assume that "victim 12" referred to Lake Tahoe nurse Donna Lass, who was missing and presumed dead. Specifically, Lass disappeared during the early morning hours of September 6, 1970. Yet, by this time, the Zodiac had already penned the Button Letter, in which he took credit for his twelfth victim. Moreover, when the killer increased his score to twelve, he explained that he had shot "a man sitting in a parked car," a likely reference to SFPD Officer Richard Radetich — regardless of whether or not you believe the claim. These circumstances suggest that Radetich was supposed to be victim twelve.

But this double claiming of victim twelve is only part of the problem. More significantly, it's literally impossible to have a value that both represented the disappearance of Donna Lass and complied with the killer's running victim tally because the *Mikado* Letter and the Crackproof Card — the two communiqués immediately before and after the disappearance of Donna Lass — both list the victim count as thirteen. In other words, the killer claimed to have killed his thirteenth victim before Lass disappeared and further claimed to have killed no additional victims after she disappeared.

Event (all 1970)	Date	First Reported	Score
The "My Name Is" Letter	April 20	April 22	10
The Dragon Card	April 28	May 1	[none]
The Button Letter	June 26	June 30	12
The Kathleen Johns Letter	July 24	October 12	[none]
The *Mikado* Letter	July 26	October 12	13
Donna Lass Disappearance	September 6	n/a	n/a
The Crackproof Card	October 6	October 12	13
The Halloween Card	October 27	October 31	14*

Table 2.1: The Zodiac's ever-increasing murder score in the proximity of "victim 12"

Some interpret these inconsistencies to mean that the Peek Through the Pines Card was not an authentic Zodiac communiqué. In my view, there's too much supporting evidence for that to be the case. We know that the killer was in the habit of continually inflating his supposed score, and that this device was primarily a taunting mechanism that had relatively little to do with his actual victim count. In this sense, the killer writing his victim count in his letters was an ongoing lie designed to create fear, uncertainty, and doubt in the minds of the people reading his written words. As is often the case when people construct ongoing lies over extended periods of time, it becomes difficult to keep track of the lies told. As conventional wisdom states, a person telling the truth can rely on what actually happened; a person telling a lie must remember what he or she said.

---

*Those who believe that the Halloween Card was a death threat and that Paul Avery was meant to be victim fourteen will argue that an implied victim count of thirteen is the proper value to use in this context.

Complicating matters in the case of the Peek Through the Pines Card are two notable factors. First, the Zodiac was referencing his victim count from more than six months earlier. In every other communication from the killer, he simply referenced the supposed score, increasing it as he saw fit. The man had his actual victims and he had his continually inflated score. Each served a purpose in the troubled mind of the killer. But how they related to each other — which victim corresponded to which number in the inflated score — mattered little, until the Peek Through the Pines Card.

The second point that may have been a contributing factor to the eventual way in which events played out is that the short-lived reporting blackout involving the coverage of Zodiac letters was in place at the time of Lass's disappearance. In particular, the arrival of the Kathleen Johns Letter and the *Mikado* Letter in July were not reported until an article on October 12, which prominently featured the Crackproof Card as well. These circumstances are relevant because it's doubtful that the killer made notes about the letters that he mailed to the newspapers. Most times he didn't have to because summaries, if not the entire text, were published within days. But during this time frame, no such summaries were forthcoming. Hence, by the time the killer sat down to construct the Crackproof Card, he likely had to rely on memory to recall what he'd written in the previous two letters. Of course, the Kathleen Johns Letter had no score. But the *Mikado* Letter did. With all the preoccupation surrounding the verbatim quoting of "I've Got a Little List" and the other interesting content in the killer's long-winded missive, he may have simply forgotten whether he'd left the score as it had been in the Button Letter a month prior or if he'd increased it.

To be sure, six months later when the killer prepared the Peek Through the Pines Card, all the information was available in the newspaper articles that he was undoubtedly saving. Whether or not he realized that there was a problem with the supposed victim count is impossible to say. Perhaps he did and dealt with the situation by choosing a number that was close enough given that no number would be perfect. Or, just as likely, he may have referred back to the *Chronicle* article from October 12, subtracted one from the victim count, and thought little more about it.

In the end, the phrase "Sought victim 12" is imperfect because of the imperfect circumstances under which it was pasted together. The implications of this imperfection are nothing more and nothing less.

* * *

Over the years, multiple people have suggested that there is some type of meaning to the single hole punched out of the Peek Through the Pines Card and its positioning on the image of the condominium project. These proposals are misguided. The value of the hole punch — both in terms of the single hole in the corner of the card and the extensive scalloping present along the edges — is abstract. As was the case with the Crackproof Card, the importance of the hole punch was its mere presence. Insofar as the location of the single hole in the Peek Through the Pines Card is concerned, the killer placed it in the return-address area on the flip side of the card and used it to create a modified Zodiac symbol. The placement of the hole on the other side of the card, the content side, was simply a matter of coincidence; it had to end up somewhere. The likelihood of the location being otherwise meaningful, especially given that the killer did not have any control over the picture published with the advertisement for the condominium project, is infinitesimal.

* * *

Finally, it's worth pointing out that both the *Los Angeles Times* Letter and the Peek Through the Pines Card marked a subtle shift in emphasis that, in retrospect, foreshadowed the killer's impending hiatus. Whereas the Zodiac's previous letters had always dealt with activities involving the immediate past or the future — for example, taking credit for a recent crime or threatening future actions — these two letters had changed focus to an event that took place half a year earlier in the case of Donna Lass's disappearance and the acknowledgment of Cheri Jo Bates's murder nearly four years prior. The killer may well have been focusing on these past events precisely because he had no recent events about which to communicate. By failing to act during the previous winter solstice and minimally commemorating the spring equinox with these two communiqués, which uncharacteristically focused on the past, the killer's diminished commitment to his previously established behavioral patterns was beginning to show. His forthcoming silence was a logical next step.

2.17   The *Exorcist* Letter | January 29, 1974

After a nearly three-year hiatus, the long-elusive fugitive from justice resurfaced to write his final authenticated letter as the Zodiac. In the months that followed, the same man likely continued to correspond a few more times. But these communiqués were from different anonymous personas: a friend, a citizen, and finally the Red Phantom. Regardless of the missives that followed, the killer could have easily omitted the *Exorcist* Letter and left his infamous persona behind in 1971. Doing nothing would have been the path of least resistance. But some aspect of the circumstances surrounding this letter compelled the man to don the mask of the Zodiac one last time. Something in the mind of the killer required him to sacrifice the comfort and safety achieved during nearly three years of inaction in order to resurrect his murderous alter ego once more. In this sense, the content of the *Exorcist* Letter had an obvious personal value to the killer that simply did not exist — at least not in the same form — in any of his other correspondence. Therefore, we should pay close attention to this letter.

> *I saw + think "The Exorcist"*
> *was the best saterical com-*
> *idy that I have ever seen.*
>
> *Signed, yours truley:*

> *He plunged him self into*
> *the billowy wave*
> *and an echo arose from*
> *the sucides grave*
> *titwillo titwillo*
> *titwillo*

The idea that *The Exorcist* — generally considered to be one of the scariest horror films of all time — was a satirical comedy is, of course, ridiculous. On the surface, this feels like the kind of absurd statement an adolescent might make for the sole purpose of garnering attention; and with the Zodiac being an attention-craving narcissist, one could argue the statement was perfectly in character. However, based on other aspects of the content, I believe it's also true that the man simply wanted to make some kind of reference to *The Exorcist*, and this was the tack that he chose.

There is, however, another possible reason for the way in which the killer chose to introduce *The Exorcist*. As mentioned in Section 9.1 of *The Zodiac Revisited, Volume 1*, Paul Avery wrote an article documenting the success and "weird goings-on" involving the movie.[50] One has to wonder if, after reading this article, the killer longed to reestablish communication with the reporter. Moreover, a quote at the beginning of the article is similar in tone to the killer's statement. Specifically, a moviegoer wanted his money back "because it was about as scary as 'Snow White.'" Perhaps the Zodiac's contrived declaration was a subtle reference to this quote in the article by his favorite reporter.

For the next section, the killer returned to quoting Ko-Ko from *The Mikado* (see Section 5.8 of *The Zodiac Revisited, Volume 1*). Specifically, the lines came from the song "Willow, Titwillow" in which Ko-Ko recounted the story of a small bird who lamented his "blighted affection" through the repeated recitation of the line "willow, titwillow, titwillow" before committing suicide. The quoted stanza was precisely the point at which the bird ended his life.

The symbolism here is obvious. The Zodiac was quoting *The Mikado* at a point in the lyrics that communicated the act of suicide. In no uncertain terms, the persona of the Zodiac was committing suicide. Or, more precisely, the man who created the persona of the Zodiac, was killing it off. This is why the world never again received an authenticated letter written by the Zodiac. The persona was dead. Moreover, this notion is further reinforced by a final instance of spatial information. By purposely positioning the suicidal lines of "Willow, Titwillow" in the area immediately following the complimentary close of the letter — the area where an author normally establishes his or her identity with a signature — the killer explicitly associated suicide with the persona's identity.

> *PS. if I do not see this*
> *note in your paper I*
> *will do something nasty,*
> *which you know I'm capable of*
> *doing*

The author made this threat out of practicality. The last thing the killer wanted to do was break his three-year silence, potentially jeopardizing his well-established safety, in order to make a public declaration that was personally important to him, only to have it be ignored or suppressed. As with other parts of the letter, this threat feels forced and uncomfortable. The phrase "which you know I'm capable of doing" comes across as a poorly executed bluff. It's as if the killer knew he was no longer capable of committing the heinous crimes he'd perpetrated in the past, but for the purposes of this letter, he needed to convince the world, and perhaps himself, that he still could.

Me–37
SFPD–0

To people familiar with the communications of the Zodiac, this missive is noteworthy for what the author chose to omit rather than what he included. In particular, gone was the ever-present introductory phrase "This is the Zodiac speaking." The ubiquitous symbol representing the killer's persona was, likewise, nowhere to be found. The introductory phrase and signature were easily avoided. However, for the score, in place of the Zodiac symbol, the killer simply wrote "Me." These circumstances are important. The man who was the Zodiac donned his murderous persona one last time for the purpose of killing it off, but he was very uncomfortable doing it. He couldn't even bring himself to draw the Zodiac symbol let alone write the phrase that he'd used to terrorize the Bay Area to such great effect. The man may have written this letter in January 1974 to publicly announce the death of the Zodiac, but the truth of the matter is that the persona had been dead long before the man put pen to paper.

Given the totality of this letter, we can begin to see the importance of *The Exorcist* and why the killer likely felt compelled to make reference to it. The story revolves around Regan, a girl who tragically becomes the victim of demonic possession. Eventually, out of desperation, her mother turns to the Catholic Church and the seldom-practiced art of exorcism. At the climax of the movie, one of the two priests performing the exorcism, Father Karras, coaxes the demon out of Regan only to have it possess his body. While still partially in control of his own faculties, the priest manages to hurl himself out of the bedroom window, thereby committing suicide and, in the process, thwarting the possession. Regan recovers and lives a happy, healthy life.

The presence of suicide in *The Exorcist* is no coincidence. Similarly, the notion of demonic possession is something that we should not casually overlook. In December 1969, the Zodiac described his condition to Melvin Belli by saying: "I cannot reach out for help because of this thing in me wont let me." Knowing this, it's easy to understand how the killer may have related to the idea of demonic possession. Furthermore, with the priest from *The Exorcist* defeating the evil of demonic possession by committing suicide and the killer referencing the film when communicating the suicide of his murderous alter ego, this too is no coincidence. The man who was the Zodiac viewed himself as having defeated the evil of his demonic possession through the symbolic act of suicide. Fortunately for him, and in stark contrast to Father Karras, the suicide in question did not require the sacrifice of his own life.

In fact, watching the film's powerful imagery and symbolism was likely the precipitating event that led him to break his long silence. Although he had long since abandoned the Zodiac persona, he was probably unsatisfied with how his alter ego had faded away without a formal end. Once he saw *The Exorcist* with its concepts and content that spoke to him in terms of his own experience, he likely believed it was the perfect time to provide the epilogue that he felt his persona deserved.

2.18   The Citizen Card | May 8, 1974

The Citizen Card offers an intriguing counter-perspective to much of the Zodiac's correspondence. The SLA Postcard from two months prior was too short to provide much substantive insight. In the Red Phantom Letter that followed two months later, the author had once again donned an assumed persona. This communiqué is unique in that it's both substantive and appears to have been written from the perspective of the man himself, without the complexity of any obvious guises.

> *Sirs–I would like to expression my ~~consterati~~ consternation concerning your poor taste + lack of sympathy for the public, as evidenced by your running of the ads for the movie "Badlands," featuring the blurb "In 1959 most people were killing time. Kit + Holly were killing people."*

Despite the childlike hand printing, this content — through its vocabulary, sentence structure, phrasing, and spelling — is indicative of an author with definite language skills. This is quite likely the most accurate representation of the author's true writing ability, as opposed to the simplistic and contrived prose found in most of the Zodiac's other correspondence.

One has to wonder if the killer's grievance with *Badlands* was really limited to the advertisement or if possibly he had seen the movie and was using the commercial as a proxy for the movie itself. In all probability, if he had seen the film, he would have found much to dislike. The story of Kit and Holly in the movie was loosely based on the real-life killing spree of Charles Starkweather and his girlfriend Caril Ann Fugate. On the surface, one might reasonably expect that an actual serial killer could relate to and, therefore, appreciate the movie's story line. But if we dig a little deeper, it's clear that Martin Sheen's character, Kit, is the exact opposite of the Zodiac in many ways. Kit is a disorganized sociopath who goes through life reacting to his circumstances. Moreover, he's good looking, charismatic, and talkative. People compare him to James Dean. He has an innate facility with the opposite sex. Holly feels special because he's chosen her, even though "he could have any girl...." And, of course, the intimate, sexual relationship between Kit and Holly is central to the entire story. Moreover, despite his murderous deeds, Kit is a genuinely likable guy. When he's finally apprehended, the law enforcement officers start out with a tough-as-nails attitude toward him. But, before long, his charismatic personality has a large contingency of the officers competing with each other, vying for the infamous criminal's attention. One of the arresting officers shakes Kit's hand and says: "I wish you luck. I sincerely mean it." The Zodiac may have had serial murder in common with the fictional Kit, but that would have been where their similarities ended.

> ... *(not that glorification of*
> *violence was ever justifiable)*

This sentence is one of the most consequential statements in all the killer's writing.

The man knew a thing or two about the "glorification of violence." From declaring Cheri Jo Bates's death "a ball," to expository ramblings such as "I like killing people because it is so much fun" and "To kill something gives me the most thrilling experience ... ," to extreme threats constructed precisely to elicit fear, for example, "I think I shall ... pick off the kiddies as they come bouncing out," to the explicit use of the word "glory," as in " ... there is more glory in killing a cop than a cid ... ," the killer, through his own written words, had covered the spectrum of violence glorification.

Relatedly, herein lies the significance of this parenthetical statement. The declaration was not a true assessment of the circumstances surrounding the advertisement of *Badlands*, but rather a self-repudiation of past deeds: a thinly veiled, indirect but nevertheless clear indication of remorse. Not only was the Zodiac persona long gone, as communicated by the *Exorcist* Letter, but the killer was expressing guilt for his criminal actions. This was an equally important part of reestablishing communication after his three-year silence. He needed to say goodbye as the Zodiac, but he also needed to communicate as himself that he had evolved to a point where he felt some degree of remorse for his previous acts of violence.*

---

*People have suggested to me that if the killer truly was a psychopath, he would have been incapable of experiencing remorse. While I understand and appreciate the point, I am not willing to abandon the conclusion because of it. Certainly, I am not a psychologist. Nevertheless, the reasons for my opinion on this matter are twofold. First, our knowledge of psychopaths in general and how they process remorse in particular is evolving, as evidenced by a 2016 research article on the subject.[51] Second, I feel an obligation to go where the evidence objectively leads, regardless of how unexpected or uncomfortable such a destination may be. In this instance, in my considered opinion, the evidence undeniably leads to the conclusion.

2.19 The Red Phantom Letter | July 8, 1974

From its modest beginnings in 1865, the *San Francisco Chronicle* quickly grew into an integral part of its namesake city. Through two catastrophic earthquakes and other tumultuous events visited upon the City by the Bay during the previous century, the *Chronicle* impressively maintained its unblemished record of never missing a day of publication.

By 1965, the *Chronicle* and the *Examiner* had been engaged in a long-standing, intense, and sometimes bitter, if not destructive, rivalry. Motivated by the promise of a healthier existence, the two powerhouse newspapers negotiated a merger whereby one would publish a morning edition, the other would operate as an afternoon paper, and the two would join forces to publish the substantial Sunday edition. With the *Chronicle* having the larger circulation, the powers that be insisted that it maintain the coveted morning edition, and the representatives of the *Examiner* acquiesced.[52] With this move, the *Chronicle* solidified its position atop the hierarchy of San Francisco's newspapers.

The state of the *Chronicle*'s existence, however, had not always been so rosy. In 1952, the newspaper found itself ranked dead last when compared with the city's three other dailies, trailing not only William Randolph Hearst's flagship *Examiner*, which boasted a circulation more than double that of the *Chronicle*, but also the *Oakland Tribune* and the *San Francisco News-Call Bulletin*.[53]

To address the situation, the owners of the *Chronicle* orchestrated a change in leadership by appointing Scott Newhall as executive editor. The flamboyant Newhall had started at the newspaper in 1934; initially a photographer, he later moved up the ranks through various editorial staffs. Once in charge, Newhall implemented his vision for an overall strategy that attacked the problem of readership from all angles. As Newhall's wife, Ruth, put it: "Scott assured me he would 'bury' the *Examiner* and then proceeded to do so."[54]

One of the approaches that Newhall championed was to introduce a significant degree of fun and entertainment into what had previously been a straightlaced newspaper. In pursuit of this end, Newhall hired a colorful personality named Marc Spinelli to write a glamour advice column under the pseudonym "Count Marco." In Newhall's words: "The column is aimed at the American wife who is approaching a more mature age, and affords her a chance to restore some of the excitement she had in her younger years."[55] More accurately, the column was intended to offend, in entertaining fashion, the sensibilities of housewives throughout the Bay Area.

Spinelli delivered. The Count Marco column debuted in 1959, and soon tens of thousands of women (and men) across the Bay Area were regularly reading Spinelli's daily installment so they could share the common bond of being mutually incensed at the man. Readers despised Count Marco so much that they continually perused his column just to see what he would say next. Newhall and Spinelli had artfully crafted a persona that people loved to hate.

By 1974, the Count Marco column had been in print for fifteen years. The persona created by Spinelli and Newhall was a well-established San Francisco personality known for, among other things, driving around the city in a pink Rolls Royce. The formula discovered so many years earlier continued to work its magic with little modification required.

This is the context that existed at the time the killer took extreme offense to something Spinelli wrote. On first consideration, the question of what, precisely, motivated the man to put pen to paper might seem nearly impossible to discern given the shortness of the Red Phantom Letter. Indeed, the Count Marco columns from the month preceding the Red Phantom Letter encompass a wide array of subject matter, much of which could have plausibly provoked the killer's ire toward the author.* Notable content from this time frame included a passing mention of *The Exorcist* and a discussion of sexual dysfunction in middle-aged men, specifically an age range that likely included the killer. But one article in particular rises above all others. It was an installment titled "Your Mirror Can Also See Inside You," and

---

*For examples, please see *zodiacrevisited.com/book/count-marco*

it appeared in the *Chronicle* on July 3. In order to truly understand the Red Phantom Letter, it's essential to read this Count Marco column, so I'm reprinting it here[†] (the emphasis present in the column is from the original):

Your Mirror Can Also See Inside You

When I wrote that psychiatrists and psychologists ruined more marriages than they saved, I wasn't surprised by the angry reaction.

I had contended that shrinks look at ordinary marriage problems as "cases," to be dissected, rearranged and deranged, leaving the "patient" totally disoriented.

What would happen if a physician examined a patient and said, "You have such and such a disease. Now do something about it," without prescribing treatment.

Mother Nature is like an oyster. She heals emotional wounds through passage of time. An oyster finds a grain of sand has forced its way into the shell. As time goes on its mucous continually covers the irritant until eventually what was a sore spot becomes a magnificent pearl.

However, if one instead took a sharp instrument and sliced the pearl in half, the only result would be to expose the original grain of sand, the irritant.

According to a report in The Chronicle, behavioral researchers have shown unmistakably that psychiatry is a very imprecise tool in diagnosing mental illness.

On specific diagnoses (labeling a patient "depressive") psychiatrists can agree among themselves only about 40 per cent of the time.

Any couple having problems in their marriage can be considered depressive. Instead of sitting down and saying

---

[†] *San Francisco Chronicle.* Newspaper index by Bell & Howell Co. Reproduced with permission of Newspaper Indexing Center, Micro Photo Division, B via Copyright Clearance Center.

simply (as he should), "Look, you two. Grow up. Marriage is a give and take proposition and one of you is taking too much," the psychiatrist takes your time and money to tell you that because your mother slapped you across the mouth once for talking back, you've hated your mother ever since and consequently hate your husband, or wife.

The best psychiatric treatment you can have is taking a long truthful look in the mirror and saying honestly to yourself, "Okay, what am I doing wrong?"

Your mirror will tell you. The basic trouble with marriages is too many of you are afraid to face the truth and hope an outsider will agree.

You don't need psychiatry. All you need is the Count Marco column.

From the most direct perspective, this Count Marco column was about psychiatry and psychology, and the killer's letter has multiple references to psychology. In particular, Spinelli railed against psychology, and the killer proclaims the Count has a "psychological disorder" and "suggests" he see a "shrink." This type of reaction was very much in line with what we know of the Zodiac through his other letters in that there was a definite element of taunting and also a bit of a sense of humor.

Another insightful question to consider is this: what, precisely, was the author's issue with Count Marco? The killer used some insulting language, but the phrase that really indicated his problem with Spinelli was: "he ... always needs to feel superior." Of all the potential columns that could have been the motivating factor, only the following line from the above column truly fits:

> *You don't need psychiatry. All you need is the Count Marco column.*

Certainly, Spinelli made a living out of finding entertaining ways to enrage Bay Area housewives, and more often than not, doing so involved a substantial dose of immodesty. But even in this context, the above statement was over the top. This was exactly the type of state-ment that would invite the criticism that the Count "always needs to feel superior."

In my estimation, the specific mention of "the Count Marco col-umn" is also meaningful. Spinelli wrote "All you need is the Count Marco column," to which the killer responds: "… cancel the Count Marco column." While one could argue that these words were a likely choice for somebody taking issue with Count Marco, I think it's more probable that the phrase was a direct response to the statement the author found offensive.

Finally, the timing of this scenario fits quite well. "Your Mirror Can Also See Inside You" was published on Wednesday, July 3. The killer had Thursday (the Fourth of July) and the long, holiday week-end to craft his response. Under these circumstances, the killer prob-ably finished and possibly mailed the letter over the weekend. This chain of events is perfectly consistent with a Monday postmark.

* * *

Let's consider this final letter in the larger context of Zodiac-related events. After his communiqués in the spring of 1971, the killer dropped out of sight. Three years later, inspired by *The Exorcist*, he reemerged to kill off his Zodiac persona. Shortly thereafter, the killer lambasted the movie *Badlands* for its "glorification of violence" and, in so doing, indirectly expressed some degree of remorse. Finally, in his swan song missive, he vehemently took issue with Count Marco for the writer's disrespect of psychology and the arrogance of the assertion "All you need is the Count Marco column."

One possible scenario that explains all of these details is that the killer sought professional psychiatric help on or around the begin-ning of his hiatus, which started in spring 1971. Given that the Belli Letter appeared to be an aborted but otherwise authentic attempt to seek help, it's not unreasonable to consider that the fugitive may have followed up with one or more additional attempts. Continuing this line of thought, under the care of a psychiatrist, the killer may well have achieved some level of control over his mental disorder which, in turn, might explain the cessation of his activities starting in 1971.

If the killer did manage to make some progress with his mental disorder through the help of psychiatric treatment, it's easy to imagine that he may have honestly valued the profession of psychiatry. The remorse evident in the Citizen Card suggests the killer may have made real progress toward understanding the depth of the destruction that his actions had wrought. He likely would have been under the ongoing care of a psychiatrist and may well have considered the relationship essential to his continued state of relative mental wellbeing. Under these circumstances, one can easily imagine the killer taking offense to Count Marco's whimsical ramblings aimed at devaluing psychiatry.

One final aspect of the Red Phantom Letter that further strengthens this idea is the extent to which the author drew parallels between himself and Count Marco. In the span of just fifty-two words, the killer made two unmistakable parallels and hinted at a third.

In the letter, the author wrote that Count Marco " ... always needs to feel superior." This accusation was remarkable considering that the man who wrote it had also previously made statements such as: "The police shall never catch me because I have been too clever for them." The author knew from experience about the need to feel superior. He may have perceived the need in Count Marco, but he had also observed the need in himself.

The author continued: "Since the Count can write anonymously, so can I ... " This parallel is explicit and unambiguous. It's also interesting because it pointed out the importance of persona. Count Marco was a persona created by Marc Spinelli. The Red Phantom was also a persona, obviously constructed by the anonymous critic specifically for the purpose of taking Count Marco to task. And, of course, lurking just beneath the surface of this communiqué was the now-defunct persona of the Zodiac.

In this context, the killer's admonition — "I suggest you refer him to a shrink" — can be interpreted as yet another parallel. In other words, the killer, with whom Count Marco has so much in common, is seeing or has seen a shrink, and, therefore, Count Marco should see one as well.

2.20 Conclusion

So there we have it. From "She was young and beautiful" — the opening line of The Confession — to "Red with rage" — the parenthetical clarification of the *Red Phantom* signature — we've examined the most meaningful elements of the communiqués commonly attributed to the man who, for a time, called himself the Zodiac. The killer's correspondence encompassed approximately 3,500 words penned over eight years starting around Thanksgiving of 1966 and ending just before the Fourth of July 1974. Some of these words have been shown to be the straightforward articulation of unsophisticated thoughts. Others, perhaps the most valuable in our analysis, have proven themselves to be meaningful in ways that are not evident on initial consideration but rather can only be understood against the backdrop of known events and in the context of related information. Finally, much to our continued dismay, some parts of the killer's communications have remained a mystery, despite our best efforts to make sense of them.

Along the way, we've seen clear foundational themes such as an obvious hatred of women (and, to a lesser extent, couples), a hatred that hints at a debilitating social dysfunction in the life of the killer. We've identified cause-and-effect stimuli and actions that paint the picture of a narcissistic villain who felt disrespected by Martin Lee and the rest of the San Francisco Police Department. We've interpreted evidence that points to the act of murder evolving from an end in and of itself into a means to the more general ends of power, control, and simple terrorism. We've come to understand how motivating factors such as certain anniversaries and *The Exorcist* likely moved the killer to the point of action on numerous occasions. Finally, we've reviewed evidence that suggests, contrary to conventional wisdom, that the killer achieved some degree of self-awareness in terms of understanding his murderous deeds, which, in turn, led him to feel some sense of remorse.

Clearly, this substantial component of our analysis, which was based on the killer's own written words, has yielded considerable insight into the as-of-yet unidentified man and his psychodynamics. While undeniably valuable, there remains yet one more dimension to our analysis that will not only complement our newfound understanding but also prove valuable in its own right.

Notes

1. "Detectives Dig Deep into Cheri Bates' Background," *The Press,* November 8, 1966, C2.

2. "Riverside City College Coed Found Murdered," *Redlands Daily Facts,* October 31, 1966, 1.

3. "RCC Coed, 18, Slain on Campus," *The Press,* October 31, 1966, A1.

4. "Coed Stabbed to Death on Riverside College Campus," *Los Angeles Times,* November 1, 1966, 3.

5. "Typed Confession Letter Receives Close Attention of Police Experts," *The Press,* November 30, 1966, B1.

6. George McEvoy, "Friends Quizzed in Slaying of Teen Pair Near Vallejo," *San Francisco Sunday Examiner & Chronicle,* December 22, 1968, A10.

7. "Woman Slain, Friend Is Shot," *San Francisco Sunday Examiner & Chronicle,* July 6, 1969, 9.

8. "Code Clue by Vallejo 'Killer' Sent Examiner," *San Francisco Examiner,* August 1, 1969, 3.

9. "Coded Clue in Murders," *San Francisco Chronicle,* August 2, 1969, 4.

10. "Police Seeking Clues in Vallejo Shootings," *Vallejo Times-Herald,* July 6, 1969, 1.

11. "Two Victims Found Lying Beside Road," *Vallejo Times-Herald,* July 5, 1969, 1.

12. "Gunshot Victim Fails to Identify Attacker," *Vallejo Times-Herald,* July 7, 1969, 1.

13. "Police Still Hunt for Shooting Clues," *Vallejo Times-Herald,* July 8, 1969, 2.

14. "Hunt Maniac in Murders of Teenagers," *Vallejo Times-Herald,* December 23, 1968, 1, 8.

15. Kelleher, Michael D. and Van Nuys, David, *"This Is the Zodiac Speaking": Into the Mind of a Serial Killer,* Westport, Connecticut: Praeger, 2002.

16. "Crimes of the Century Production Notes," 1988, Accessed November 25, 2020, *http://zodiacrevisited.com/book/zk-cotc-armstrong.*

17. William Flynn, "Sex Fiend Sought for Six Killings," *San Francisco Examiner,* October 1, 1969, 6.

18. Malcolm Glover, "Hundreds of 'Zodiac' Tips Flood Bay Police," *San Francisco Examiner,* October 18, 1969, 1.

19. Paul Avery, "Zodiac — Portrait of the Killer," *San Francisco Chronicle*, October 18, 1969, 1.

20. *Unsub; Vallejo Times Herald, Vallejo, California — Victim, Extortion, OO: Sacramento*, Internal Correspondence (Teletype), Federal Bureau of Investigation, Sacramento Field Office, November 14, 1969.

21. "Police Clear Zodiac Suspect at Las Vegas," *San Francisco Examiner*, October 31, 1969, 17.

22. Johns, Kathleen, interview by Johnny Smith and Howard Davis, "H. J. N. Terprises, Inc.," January 1, 1998, audio recording.

23. Paul Avery, "The Search for Zodiac's 4 Weapons," *San Francisco Chronicle*, October 22, 1969, 1.

24. "I've Killed Seven, The Zodiac Claims," *San Francisco Chronicle*, November 12, 1969, 1.

25. Paul Avery, "Fear Rides the Yellow Bus," *San Francisco Chronicle*, October 21, 1969, 5.

26. "FBI Checks for Clue in Slaying," *San Francisco Chronicle*, October 2, 1969, 2.

27. "Message to the Zodiac Killer," *San Francisco Sunday Examiner & Chronicle*, October 19, 1969, A1.

28. "To the Zodiac," *San Francisco Examiner*, October 21, 1969, 1.

29. "A Message To Zodiac," *San Francisco Examiner*, October 22, 1969, 8.

30. Will Stevens, "Cipher Expert Dares Zodiac to 'Tell' Name," *San Francisco Examiner*, October 22, 1969, 9.

31. Don Branning, "'Zodiac' Boasts of 10 Killings," *San Francisco Examiner*, October 22, 1970, 18.

32. Paul Avery, "Zodiac Sends New Letter — Claims Ten," *San Francisco Chronicle*, April 22, 1970, 1.

33. Paul Avery, "Yellow Cab Sets Reward for Zodiac," *San Francisco Chronicle*, January 28, 1970, 4.

34. Guy Wright, "Fan Letter for Dave Toschi," *San Francisco Sunday Examiner & Chronicle*, July 23, 1978, B3.

35. "Bullets in Bomb That Killed Sgt. McDonnell," *San Francisco Examiner*, March 23, 1970, 4.

36. "Rode with Zodiac, Woman Claims," *San Francisco Examiner*, March 23, 1970, 4.

37. "It Was a Very Wet Week Here," *Cupertino Courier*, January 14, 1970, 6.

38. "Weather: Wet and Dark, Too," *Cupertino Courier*, January 21, 1970, 2.

39. Ricardo Eugirtni Gomez, "Preliminary Report on Project MK-ZODIAC: 1228," 2009, Accessed November 25, 2020, *http://zodiacrevisited.com/book/gomez-belli*.

40. Paul Avery, "Belli Sure Zodiac Will Talk to Him," *San Francisco Chronicle*, December 30, 1969, 3.

41. "4 Join Hunt for 'Cipher Killer,'" *San Francisco Examiner*, October 4, 1969, 3.

42. "Zodiac Halloween Threat," *San Francisco Chronicle*, October 31, 1970, 1.

43. Accessed, November 25, 2020, *http://zodiacrevisited.com/book/dictionary-doom*.

44. Dave Smith, "17-Plus Victims Claimed in Letter by Zodiac Killer," *Los Angeles Times*, March 16, 1971, 3.

45. Paul Avery, "Zodiac Writes Again — '17 Dead,'" *San Francisco Chronicle*, March 16, 1971, 1.

46. "Couple Found Slain on Secluded Beach," *Los Angeles Times*, June 7, 1963, 1.

47. "Slayer of Newlyweds Hunted," *Los Angeles Times*, February 7, 1964, 1.

48. Arthur Berman, "Honeymooner Killings Called Maniac's Work," *Los Angeles Times*, February 8, 1964, 1.

49. "Suspect Held in 1963 Sweethearts' Slaying," *Los Angeles Times*, December 3, 1964, A1.

50. Paul Avery, "Weird Goings-on at the Movies," *San Francisco Chronicle*, January 11, 1974, 1.

51. Arielle Baskin-Sommers, Stuppy-Sullivana Allison M, and Joshua W. Buckholtz, "Psychopathic Individuals Exhibit but Do Not Avoid Regret During Counterfactual Decision Making," *Proceedings of the National Academy of Sciences of the United States of America*, December 2016, Accessed November 25, 2020, *http://zodiacrevisited.com/book/pnas-2016-12*.

52. "Newspapers: Survival, not Sentiment," *Time*, September 17, 1965.

53. Cynthia Gorney, "The State of The American Newspaper — The Battle of the Bay," *American Journalism Review*, January 1999, Accessed November 25, 2020, *http://zodiacrevisited.com/book/web-newall-2*.

54. Ruth Waldo Newhall, "The Life And Times of Scott Newhall," *Old Town Newhall Gazette*, January 1996, Accessed November 25, 2020, *http://zodiacrevisited.com/book/web-newhall-1*.

55. "The Press: Voice from the Sewer," *Time*, August 12, 1959.

3

Reconsidering the Crimes

We discriminate at first only a few features, and we need to reconsider our experience from many points of view and in various moods, to preserve the whole fruit of it.

Henry David Thoreau, 1817–1862

Having reviewed the facts of the case, analyzed the individual themes woven through its fabric, and reconsidered the written words attributed to the killer, we are now in a position to reexamine the crimes themselves in order to develop a more thorough understanding. Additionally, the review of each crime includes a Speculative Evolution section in which I theorize as to what events may have preceded or followed the killer's criminal actions. These sections are based in fact, but, as the name implies, they include a significant degree of speculation. The proposed scenarios explain the facts as we know them and are helpful in terms of developing a high-level understanding of the killer. Nevertheless, they are ultimately and analytical tool. Other circumstances and scenarios are certainly possible.

3.1   Robert Domingos and Linda Edwards
June 4, 1963

The murder of these high school sweethearts has many of the hallmarks of an initial homicide. There are no earlier murders that clearly fit the killer's known modus operandi or signature. Several clues at the crime scene indicated inexperience, including the botched attempt at burning down the beach shack, the four boxes of ammunition left behind, and a perpetrator who fired his weapon at least twenty-six times, perhaps out of panic. Furthermore, the fact that the killer likely lost control of the situation as he had one victim tie up the other demonstrates that events unfolded in an unanticipated way. While there is clear evidence of substantial premeditation, even in this crime — precut lengths of rope, a secluded crime scene, profiled victim selection, etc. — the fact that the killer lost control of his victims suggests the premeditated situational control that would come to characterize many of his later crimes was either immature or nonexistent at this point in his criminal evolution. In fact, it might have been this very experience that motivated the killer to make premeditated situational control a key element of any future crimes involving significant victim interaction. And more specifically, the problems encountered in Gaviota may have translated to the practical reasons why the killer felt the need to wear a disguise at Lake Berryessa — he had already seen how easily plans can fall apart.

If the killer was responsible for these murders and he'd progressed in a manner similar to other organized serial killers, we might expect that he resided somewhere in the vicinity of Gaviota, assuming these were, indeed, his first homicides. The idea behind this suggestion is that he would have started in an area where he was comfortable and expanded outwardly as he gained experience and increased his criminal sophistication.[1] However, given what we know about the remainder of his crimes, it's unlikely. All three Southern California attacks required a high degree of premeditation and planning. In all three cases, the crimes were carried out in secluded locations that the killer likely chose for their isolation. In some respects, whom he killed was less important than where he killed. The victims were symbolic and, hence, any number of couples (or a woman, in the case of Cheri Jo Bates) could have satisfied the killer's psychological needs. The location, however, had to be frequented by the appropriate victim type *and* it had to satisfy many constraints that enabled the perpetration of the crime. With the next murders occurring 250 miles away in San Diego, it's unlikely that the man would have driven so far — roughly five hours — committed the crime, and returned to the area of his residence. A much more likely scenario, which is otherwise consistent with what we know about the crimes, is that the man resolved to commit these murders some distance away from his actual residence from the outset and then drove a considerable distance to both Gaviota and San Diego. As such, we should expect that the killer's residence, generally speaking, would have been somewhere between the two. Extending this line of thought to Riverside continues to make sense in that the town is located between Gaviota and San Diego (from a north-south perspective), but it is further inland to the east. In fact, if we triangulate these three crime scenes, see Figure 3.1, it is likely that the killer lived somewhere within the borders of this triangle, although probably not too close (perhaps fifty miles) to any of the crime scenes. This triangle includes the Greater Los Angeles area as well as other well-populated Southern California localities.

A corollary to this interpretation diminishes the value of the boxes of ammunition found at the Gaviota crime scene. Detectives did an impressive job of investigating the crime, including tracking down the possible sources of the four boxes of Winchester Super-X .22-caliber long-rifle ammunition bearing lot number TL21. However, their understandable conclusion that the boxes probably came from the PX at Vandenberg Air Force Base was built upon the assumption that the ammunition had been purchased locally. Under the scenario described above, the killer could have purchased the ammunition anywhere in Southern California, if not elsewhere.

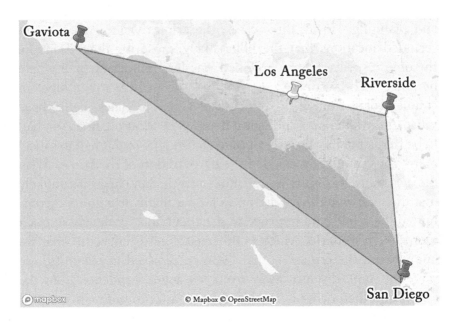

Figure 3.1: The triangle formed by the three Southern California crime scenes. Likely the killer lived somewhere within this region during the time of the Southern California crimes, possibly in the Greater Los Angeles area.

In the aftermath of the Gaviota murders, the person who had an immediate and uncanny insight into what he was dealing with was Santa Barbara County Sheriff James Webster. He recognized the perpetrator as a psychopath whose actions defied normal motive. He would soon aptly label the fugitive a "Sweetheart Slayer." However, the killer was already benefiting from his choice of stranger murder, his self-imposed requirement that he travel a considerable distance, and the fact that he had preyed upon a couple that was younger than him. The investigation, understandably, was generating a litany of possible suspects who were all similar in age to the victims. Soon after, the investigation was fundamentally confused as the result of the search for the mysterious "beachcomber." Though clouded by this investigative distraction, Sheriff Webster was still correct in his basic understanding of the nature of the fugitive for whom he was searching. Just months after the Gaviota murders, Webster warned surrounding areas that the "psychotic" and "motiveless" killer may well surface elsewhere along the coast to prey upon lovestruck couples. Of course, his insight would soon prove prescient.

3.1.1 Speculative Evolution

In all likelihood, the man who would later be known as the Zodiac lived in the Greater Los Angeles area in early 1963. As a psychopath tormented by an inability to form meaningful adult relationships, especially intimate relationships with women, he probably indulged in fantasies about lashing out against the symbol of his dysfunction, namely couples — but not just any couple under any circumstance. For his message to be clear, his fantasies centered around young and happy couples — a handsome man paired with a loving and beautiful woman. The type of couple whom anybody might look upon and secretly harbor more than a hint of jealousy. The type of couple for whom good things just happen naturally. And importantly, the type of couple that the killer could never have been a part of.

Sometime in the spring of 1963, the man's fantasies had become so intense that he felt compelled to act. His mental disorder notwithstanding, the man possessed significant intelligence and a firm grasp on reality. Consequently, he began to plan his initial attack by scouting potential sites. Each site needed to: (a) be some distance from his residence, (b) be frequented by lone couples, and (c) possess a romantic isolation so as to send the correct message and also accommodate the perpetration of the crime. With these goals in mind, the killer likely drove north on Highway 101. In the weeks preceding the initial attack, the killer probably identified one or more such sites, including the one at Gaviota. He also may have set out with the intent to kill one or more times prior to June 4 but failed to find reasonable victims under accommodating circumstances, and the man had the mental discipline to wait for the right opportunity. Finally, on the Lompoc High School Senior Ditch Day, the unknown subject's planning came to its fruition when he found a single car — that of Robert

Domingos — parked on the median of Highway 101. The man likely surveyed the situation and, after convincing himself that he'd found suitable victims, he grabbed his weapons, ammunition, and precut lengths of rope and trekked down to the ocean's shore. By the time he returned to his vehicle, he had crossed the line that divides those of us who are normal, contributing members of society from the murderers among us.

As stated earlier, the commission of the crime that took the lives of Robert Domingos and Linda Edwards did not go according to plan. Whatever morbid fantasy the man had in store for the couple had he managed to tie them up was thwarted. Santa Barbara County Detective William Baker, who inherited the case and discovered the likely connection involving the Zodiac, believed the man intended to do to Domingos and Edwards what he later did to Bryan Hartnell and Cecelia Sheppard at Lake Berryessa. That appears to be the most logical conclusion. Beyond the killer's unrealized intentions, however, there were a number of other mistakes, any one of which could have led law enforcement straight to the killer. But the man got lucky; he got away with it. He had survived the commission of his first murders, mistakes and all, and gained valuable experience that would, to society's detriment, enable him to be a more effective murderer in the future.

In the days that followed the murders, the killer certainly relished the attention that the *Los Angeles Times*, television, and radio paid to his murderous deeds. He likely made some efforts to obtain copies of the *Santa Barbara News-Press*, which covered the investigation most thoroughly, but he would have had to have been exceptionally careful not to draw attention to himself in the process. He likely would not have bought the newspaper through any means that required human interaction, and he probably had limited opportunities to drive the distance needed to purchase the newspaper from a vending machine. Later, he would learn to extend the dark satisfaction he derived from the news reports through the act of writing letters. But, for the time being, he was still adjusting to his new role as a depraved murderer.

3.2 Johnny Ray Swindle and Joyce Swindle February 5, 1964

The most notable characteristic of the murders of Joyce and Johnny Ray Swindle in San Diego is the extent to which the location of the crime facilitated the commission of the murders. As discussed earlier in Section 1.1.3, this accommodation was not the result of happenstance; it was the product of significant premeditation. Moreover, this specific crime scene — with its highly functional sniper's nest and its elevated level of ambient noise* — provides compelling evidence that this particular location was more important than the chosen victims. The killer was not following the Swindles; he wasn't targeting them. He would have been just as satisfied to gun down any other lovestruck couple on that February evening in 1964. Even more clearly than in the case of the Gaviota murders, these victims were symbolic. Johnny Ray and Joyce Swindle were, quite literally, in the wrong place at the wrong time. Sadly, fate required that the couple pay with their lives for having had this misfortune.

As the Gaviota investigation became confused by its beachcomber tangent, people began to dismiss the likelihood that the two crimes were connected.[2] By the time detectives found, interviewed, and cleared George Gill* — ten months after the San Diego murders — the will to reconsider and reestablish the probable connection between the two crimes had evaporated. Once again, the manner in which the killer orchestrated the crimes, especially his use of different weapons, was paying dividends, this time in terms of clouding the linkage.

It's impossible to know whether the killer had the foresight to use a different weapon in San Diego specifically to frustrate attempts at

---

*A couple in a car two blocks away reported not hearing anything over the "roar of the surf."[2]

*The mysterious "beachcomber" was a flawed amalgam of George Gill — the man who built and lived in the shack where the bodies of Robert Domingos and Linda Edwards were found — and the so-called Sandy suspect. See Section 8.1 of *The Zodiac Revisited, Volume 1.*

linking the crime to Gaviota or if his choice was the result of some other motivation. Regardless, one thing is certain. By the time public reaction to the San Diego murders faded, the killer undoubtedly understood that the primary reason law enforcement was unable to connect the two crimes was due to his use of different weapons.

As we've seen with multiple homicides in the extended cases of the Zodiac, investigations of stranger murder are significantly affected by the particular strangers who are murdered. With popular people like Darlene Ferrin or, to a slightly lesser extent, Robert Domingos and Linda Edwards, the multitude of relationships in the victims' lives translated into a multitude of possible suspects. At the other end of the spectrum are victims like the Swindles. Joyce had been in San Diego for only a week, and Johnny Ray was a quiet guy who tended to keep to himself when he wasn't deployed. For these reasons, in addition to the input provided by Sheriff Webster, authorities in San Diego quickly surmised that they were dealing with a psychopathic sweetheart slayer who was otherwise operating in a motiveless manner — even given the theft of Johnny Ray's wallet and watch.

3.2.1   Speculative Evolution

The perverse excitement of his first murders and the satisfaction gained by the symbolic attack on society that they represented placated the killer for a while. He probably experienced some anxiety over the numerous mistakes he'd made, but as the days turned to weeks and the weeks to months, the concern dissipated. The man was clearly more cautious and deliberate than some of history's other organized* serial killers such as Ted Bundy or Edmund Kemper (who were eventually apprehended). Nevertheless, likely sometime in the summer or fall of 1963, his thoughts turned to his next act.

---

*Criminal profilers broadly classify serial killers as either organized or disorganized. The man who became the Zodiac was clearly an organized serial killer, as exemplified by his high degree of premeditation.

Having driven some distance north to find the Gaviota location, the killer decided to minimize the likelihood of being connected to his first crime by venturing in the opposite direction to find a viable location for his next attack. Again, due to the symbolism involved, he continued to target lovestruck couples. With these thoughts in mind, he headed south to identify potential attack sites. Possibly because of his experience in Gaviota, or the characteristics of the attack sites he was finding, or to minimize the chance of law enforcement linking his crimes, the killer opted to modify his modus operandi and simply shoot his victims with his weapon of choice, a .22-caliber rifle. Wanting to fire his weapon far fewer times than he had in Gaviota, the man decided to use hollow-point bullets, which he knew would maximize his damage and increase his lethality. Through some channel, likely chosen for its difficult traceability, the killer obtained the ammunition.

San Diego likely struck the man as a good choice because it's a military city, and, as such, the environment could have erroneously suggested that the crime was committed by a member of the armed services. Through one or more trips, he eventually found the ideal sniper location that provided substantial cover while also allowing him to identify potential victims enjoying a nighttime stroll along the beach. He probably made one or more practice runs, likely without his weapon, to verify that the site would yield victims matching his desired profile.

Having convinced himself that all the pieces were in place, he set out with the intention of perpetrating his second assault on society. Again, if the opportunity did not present itself under accommodating circumstances, the killer possessed the mental discipline to abort the mission and try again on another occasion. However, as likely as not, Wednesday, February 5, 1964, was his first such outing made with a true intention to kill.

Whether or not the killer was employed, and if so in what capacity, remains unclear. However, it's possible that he set out for his destination after a normal workday at a nine-to-five type job. More likely, he had a job with unconventional work hours. Either way, he made the drive to San Diego and arrived at his sniper's nest, weapon in hand, by 8:00 p.m. — possibly earlier, but certainly not before dark. When the Swindles approached at roughly 8:15 p.m., he deemed the circumstances acceptable and took action. The fact that the couple had begun celebrating their love for each other by sharing the Valentine's Day candy Johnny Ray had bought must have been a poignancy for which the killer couldn't have dared to hope.

After the killer incapacitated his victims, he left the concealment of his makeshift sniper's nest and, as he'd done in Gaviota, shot each victim at point-blank range. However, unlike Gaviota, he took some personal effects from one of his victims, namely Johnny Ray's wallet and watch. This was likely done to confuse the investigation by suggesting a possible, but erroneous, motive of robbery. In this sense, the killer's criminal sophistication was evolving. Additionally, or possibly alternatively, he may have taken the possessions as souvenirs to help him remember or relive his murderous exploits, as serial killers are known to do.

With the deed done, the killer quickly made his way to his vehicle and headed home. In the days that followed, he certainly paid close attention to the reporting in the *Los Angeles Times*. Again, he may have attempted to obtain copies of the *San Diego Union* to get more detailed information about the investigation. Of course, he would've maintained his extreme caution in doing so. Nonetheless, he was likely more successful than he was with Gaviota, since the *San Diego Union* is a more prominent newspaper than the *Santa Barbara News-Press*.

3.3 Cheri Jo Bates | October 30, 1966

For years, if not decades, most people who were knowledgeable about the Zodiac case believed the same man killed Cheri Jo Bates. Paul Avery's discovery of the Riverside crime that bore such clear similarity to the Zodiac's behavior, Sherwood Morrill's handwriting authentication, and the Zodiac's claim of responsibility all seemed to reinforce the obvious. Even the Riverside Police Department was on board early on. However, as was the case with Kathleen Johns, the passage of time and the absence of investigative progress conspired to cast doubt on the connection. Nurtured by the RPD's belief in a local suspect, subsequent inconclusive handwriting analysis, and the increased popularity of the Taking Credit theory, many people began to view the Zodiac's reference to his "Riverside activity" as just a bit of opportunism.

The letter writing following Cheri's homicide is a difficult point to reconcile for those who doubt her murderer and the Zodiac were one and the same. People whom I know and respect surmise that the Bay Area killer wrote the six-month anniversary notes and even The Confession but did not actually commit the murder. These scenarios are hard to accept.

Murder rate clearances in the 1960s were above 90 percent. The increased prevalence of stranger murder that would come to characterize subsequent decades was practically unheard of at the time — in some sense, the Zodiac was a precursor of things to come. Consequently, most murders were committed by people known to the victim, and most were solved with relatively straightforward police work. This is evident in the fact that Riverside had no unsolved homicides on its books prior to Cheri's murder.

The poem that an RCC janitor found scrawled on the varnished wood of a library study desk was yet another troubling piece of evidence. The only reason authorities initially thought the poem might be related to the crime was its morbid content. But that same morbid content was an imperfect match to the act of violence that took Cheri's life. In the poem, the woman was wearing a red dress. The author asserted: "she won't die this time Someone'll find her." Moreover, with the title "Sick of living / unwilling to die," the poem seemed to be more about suicide than murder. In fact, the only reason the poem became so deeply embedded into the evidence of the case is that Sherwood Morrill claimed the desktop writing was a match to the envelopes of the six-month anniversary notes. Two things bother me about this. One, as much as it troubles me to say, I believe Morrill may have been unduly influenced by Paul Avery's opinion and the apparent totality of the situation. Morrill would not have even analyzed the envelopes and the desktop poem had it not been for Avery's work. The *Chronicle* reporter, before Morrill's thorough analysis, described the two writing samples by saying: "the printing on the ... envelopes seemed to match exactly the desk poem writing."[3] After his preliminary examination, Morrill explained away the "minor differences" by suggesting that they were due to the killer's "ever-worsening mental condition."[4] However, by the next day, California's top document examiner had concluded: "The handprinting scratched on the desk is the same as on the three letters, particularly like that on the envelopes...."

There are differences between the two writing samples. While I have no qualifications as a document examiner, I do challenge Avery's characterization that the writing "seemed to match exactly." Furthermore, defacing a wood surface with a ballpoint pen is a difficult task, which yields writing that is disconnected and uncharacteristic of the writer. Undoubtedly, this contributed to the author of the poem choosing to print in the way that he or she did. The author of the six-month anniversary notes and their corresponding envelopes chose to use a contrived printing style that was intended to mask the characteristics of his true writing. I suspect these two facts may have combined to complicate the analysis of the handwriting and to suggest a connection between the two when, in fact, no such connection existed.

As detailed in Section 1.3, the anniversary notes have behavioral elements that reinforced their connection to the Zodiac. They were written as three perspective-adjusted letters, just as the Zodiac wrote his initial letters. The notes taunted law enforcement and the community's newspaper, actions that would soon define the Zodiac. The note to Cheri's father demonstrated an unmistakable and cruel desire to torment one of the people who'd been emotionally devastated by the crime, a behavior that the Zodiac later exhibited with Kathleen Johns and Mary Pilker (Donna Lass's sister). On the other hand, apart from Morrill's analysis — which is disputed — there was no significant reason to connect the desktop poem to the Zodiac. Hence, I suggest the poem was just one of many red herrings in the case, distracting us from the elements of analysis that truly deserve our attention.

The paint-spattered Timex watch found at the scene of Cheri's murder seemed like it had the potential to be a valuable clue. Early on, investigators were able to determine that the watch had been purchased from a post exchange at an overseas military base.[5] The RPD published a picture of the watch and asked for the public's help in identifying its owner,[6] but no useful information is known to have resulted from the effort.

Of course, the common assumption is that Cheri managed to rip the watch from the killer's wrist during her final moments of life. However, another possibility exists. If we search the case evidence in the extended crimes of the Zodiac, we don't have to look very far in order to turn up a plausible and intriguing explanation.

Johnny Ray Swindle was a Radioman Third Class in the US Navy who, in the years prior to his murder, served aboard a destroyer. He likely would have had the opportunity to acquire a wristwatch at a post exchange of an overseas military base. Moreover, Johnny Ray spent the last day of his life *painting* the interior of an apartment for his landlord. Although not initially disclosed, two and a half weeks after Johnny Ray and Joyce Swindle were inexplicably gunned down, San Diego Police revealed that Johnny Ray's wallet and his *watch* were missing and had almost certainly been taken by the killer.[7]

In summary, a likely paint-spattered timepiece was taken from a military victim who was known to have served aboard one of the US Navy's destroyers. Then, at the very next crime in the chronology, a paint-spattered watch that was apparently purchased by a member of the military while overseas was found at the scene of the crime. This is too much coincidence to dismiss as mere happenstance.

The obvious possible explanation is that the killer took Johnny Ray's watch and then left it to be discovered near Cheri's lifeless body, with the wristband torn so as to look like it came off during the struggle. This was likely a calculated bit of investigatory misdirection.

Just as taking the wallet and watch was an escalation in the killer's criminal sophistication — it provided for the possibility of an alternative motive — the use of the watch as a fake clue that could possibly derail the investigation was likely yet another escalation.

3.3.1   Speculative Evolution

If the killer was, indeed, following the media coverage after the murder of the Swindles, he would've known that Sheriff Webster was on to him. For his second murder, the killer had selected a location that was 250 miles away from his first. Not only had Sheriff Webster immediately recognized the work of the killer, but it came out that Sheriff Webster had predicted the killer's action. One thing was for sure, if the killer murdered another couple under similar circumstances, law enforcement would immediately suspect him and the event would reenforce the connection between the Gaviota and San Diego crimes.

Confronted with this reality, and possibly temporarily satisfied with the progress he'd made lashing out at the couples of the world, the killer decided to lay low for a while. He probably considered continuing his symbolic assault on couples farther away from the previous crime scenes or possibly under different circumstances, but ultimately, he concluded that it was not worth the risk. There's also the possibility that some aspect of the San Diego crime scared him into believing he was almost caught, which further pushed him to the point of inaction.

Eventually, the man's mental pathology overrode his caution, and he was once again compelled to act. This time, however, in order to avoid the unwanted attention of Sheriff Webster, he changed a few aspects of his crime. Instead of targeting a couple, he focused his deadly intentions on the type of individual at the center of his hatred: a young, desirable woman. To further minimize the similarities to his previous crimes, he changed his weapon of choice from a .22-caliber gun to a knife. Finally, he abandoned the idea of attacking on a beach and instead moved inland, although still targeting an area some distance from his residence. He likely felt that these differences would be enough to prevent Sheriff Webster from recognizing the crime.

The killer must have known that attacking an unknown woman with a knife in public would be difficult. He realized that he'd need some kind of manipulation scheme to ensnare his victim. Although he almost certainly recognized the need for such a scheme after the botched Gaviota murders, this crime was the first one in which he actually utilized the premeditated situational control that would characterize many of his later crimes. Based on his personal experience and his knowledge of automobiles, he conceived of the ruse that we know he used. (For additional details, see *The Zodiac Revisited, Volume 1*, Section 6.1.)

With a general idea of what he planned, the killer began the task of locating a viable attack site. He'd gone north and south previously, so this time, he decided to move inland. Driving east of Los Angeles, he looked for his next crime scene. The killer needed to find a place where beautiful, young women would drive alone. After giving the subject some thought and exploring various areas, he came up with the idea of a community college. It was a perfect match. There would be female students, and at a community college, none of the students would live on campus, so many of them would drive. With these thoughts in mind, he eventually found the Riverside Community College library, which seemed to satisfy the requirements exceptionally well. Not only did the location fit the criteria described above, but it was also right next to two abandoned houses. He figured he could easily take his victim to this area with little chance of being disturbed.

As he likely did with his previous attacks, the killer made one or more trial runs to stake out the library and convince himself that the location had the potential to yield the desired victim under accommodating circumstances. He also became familiar with the library's hours, including its odd Sunday schedule of being closed from 5:00 to 6:00 p.m. At 1:00 a.m. on Sunday, October 30, Daylight Saving Time ended, which meant it would get dark an hour earlier. Indeed, on this particular day, the sun would set at 5:00 p.m., so by the time the library reopened, it would be dark. The killer may have opted to wait for this change, or it may have been just a coincidence.

Sometime in the middle of that Sunday afternoon, the assailant left his residence, driven by an intention to kill. He arrived at the library and waited for a victim. Sadly, it was Cheri who attracted his attention when she parked her lime-green Volkswagen and entered the library just after it reopened. Under the cover of darkness, the man made his move.

From the killer's perspective, the fact that Cheri drove a Volkswagen Beetle was a stroke of good luck. Not only could the engine compartment be accessed even if the car was locked,* but the killer could access it less conspicuously because the engine was located in the rear of the vehicle.

Since nobody could say for sure that they'd seen Cheri in the library, she likely spent relatively little time inside, albeit long enough to allow the assailant to sabotage her vehicle. After Cheri spent a few minutes trying to start her car, the man approached, masking his psychopathy and true intentions with a good impression of congeniality. Having limited knowledge of automotive operation, Cheri was happy to have the help. After building trust through a few feigned attempts at fixing the car, the man made some bogus diagnosis and moved on to the next stage of his plan. Likely, he used some kind of additional ruse to get Cheri to go with him, for example, saying she can use his phone, or he'd give her a ride. Once removed from the scene, he took control of the situation, likely with a gun. From what we know about other instances of his premeditated situational control, he probably used yet another ruse to elicit the desired response, such as telling her

---

*Cheri's vehicle was a 1960 Volkswagen Beetle. At the time, it was possible to factory order a Beetle with a locking decklid (engine compartment cover). Also, a Volkswagen dealership could replace a non-locking latch with a locking one. Nevertheless, the vast majority of Beetles were manufactured without a locking decklid and were never upgraded.

I would like to thank Volkswagen Beetle experts Eric Shoemaker, Jay Salser, and David Brown for their help in understanding these circumstances.

something along the lines of: "I will kill you if I have to, but I don't want to. If you scream or try to run, you will die. But if you wait quietly with me until 11 o'clock, I'll let you go, unharmed. That is the situation. I cannot tell you anything more." Under the duress of extreme fear and confusion, Cheri would have felt she had few options and chose to cooperate accordingly.

At approximately 10:15 p.m., well after the library had closed, the killer concluded that sufficient time had passed. He took his knife and tragically ended Cheri's short life. As we know, she refused to go quietly, putting up a struggle that, in no uncertain terms, showed how much she wanted to live. But, in the end, her will to live was no match for the physical strength and weaponry of her assailant. The man injected an element of misdirection into the investigation by discarding Johnny Ray Swindle's watch. Then he quickly got into his car and drove off, having sown the seeds that would bear the fruit of frustration for decades to come.

In what was becoming a bit of a routine by this point in time, the killer likely paid close attention to the *Los Angeles Times* for news of his story. But he was probably disappointed to learn that, for the first time, the article covering his murderous exploits did not garner front-page coverage; instead the paper's editors relegated the story to page 3.[8] Because Riverside was closer to his home than the previous two crime scenes, he likely managed to get copies of the Riverside *Press* (the morning edition) or alternatively the *Enterprise* (the evening version). He was undoubtedly satisfied with the more thorough coverage found in the local papers.

It's impossible to know precisely when the killer conceived of communicating with law enforcement and the press. It may have occurred to him during his pre-crime fantasies. Given the two and a half years between the murders in San Diego and Riverside, this is the most probable scenario. He may have even decided to do it partially to influence the media's narrative and further distance himself from his other murders. Alternatively, he may have thought to write The Confession only after he committed the crime. Which way it actually happened is simply unknowable. However, from an evolutionary perspective, the timing of this change in behavior fits well. For his first two double-homicides, the killer was consumed by the crimes themselves. He was worried about getting away with it, and he was caught up in the details of perpetrating the crimes. But by the time the man was planning the Riverside murder, he had gained confidence. He'd already gotten away with the murder of four people over the course of two separate crimes. The killer had reached a point where the novelty was wearing off. He needed some way to up the ante to achieve an equivalent level of perverse excitement. He needed more.

Sometime before writing The Confession, the unknown subject made one or more telephone calls to the Riverside Police Department, undoubtedly from a pay phone. He likely traveled to Riverside (or some other location a fair distance from his home) to make the calls. The RPD apparently did not understand or appreciate the significance of the phone calls. Little in their collective experience would have prepared them for a killer as enigmatic as the one who took Cheri's life. As noted, Riverside had no unsolved murders at the time of Cheri's death. Therefore, the police had no reason to expect they would have to deal with such a scenario. Undoubtedly, the killer eventually became frustrated with the limited amount of attention that his phone calls received. These circumstances would shape his future telephonic interactions with law enforcement. But, at the time, they were simply a source of frustration for the killer.

Likely over Thanksgiving weekend of 1966, the man sat down to create what he considered his masterpiece: The Confession. The first question he had to answer: to whom should he write? Not having previously considered the question, he answered it by simply considering his audience, which consisted of two distinct groups: law enforcement and the public. For the former, he decided to write to the Riverside Police Department directly; for the latter, he opted to send a copy to the Riverside *Press–Enterprise*. He was probably wary of his handwriting being identified through some means, so he typed the letter and used multiple layers of carbon copy, sending a couple of the final copies. As intended, this process obscured any notable characteristics of his typewriter. For the envelopes, he used a felt-tip pen and block-style printing in an attempt to conceal his true handwriting. Using a style that the Zodiac would employ just three years later, he made the capital letter *I* look like a large lowercase *i* and instead of dotting the i's, he used circles. There wasn't much writing on the envelopes, so he would not have been too worried about this small sample of contrived handwriting.

For some reason, possibly to minimize forensic evidence, the man mailed the letters without stamps. On Tuesday, November 29,[*] he drove to Riverside and dropped the letters into a mailbox in time to be postmarked that afternoon. Then he returned home to wait.

On November 30, the Riverside *Press–Enterprise* published an article reviewing the progress of the homicide investigation. The killer was undoubtedly pleased to see a piece documenting the arrival of The Confession running alongside the retrospective story.[9,10] Moreover, in the days that followed, he was probably tremendously satisfied with the additional media coverage. The Confession generated nearly as much attention as the crime itself, and it had been much easier. From this point forward, the killer resolved to write letters in conjunction with his murders to heighten the satisfaction he felt.

The only problem was that if he sent letters following his crimes, it would be patently obvious that the same person was responsible. Sheriff Webster was already connecting the dots even without any letters.

Additionally, in the wake of The Confession — the killer's first foray into taunting through communication — a few refinements became obvious. First, sending a copy of the letter to the police was a waste of time. Law enforcement had little incentive to publish their version of any communication. The press, on the other hand, was

---

[*]Coincidentally, this was the same day of the week on which Robert Domingos and Linda Edwards were murdered. Perhaps the killer's nonconventional work hours included having Tuesdays off.

always motivated to publish. Furthermore, the police would get a copy of any communiqué sent to the press. Therefore, going forward, communicating with newspapers would be sufficient. Second, not including postage on the letters was a mistake. Doing so forced the letters to be routed through postal authorities instead of being delivered to the intended recipients. Whatever his reasoning for not initially including postage, the killer learned his lesson. In the near future, the Zodiac would typically use more than the required postage on his correspondence in order to guarantee normal handling.

As the investigation into Cheri's death stagnated and the memory of the ordeal began to fade from public consciousness, the killer was compelled to taunt one last time before moving on. He crafted three copies of a short letter that essentially said: "Bates had to die. There will be more." He then sent the letters to the Riverside *Press-Enterprise*, the Riverside Police Department, and Cheri's father, Joseph Bates—likely getting Joseph Bates's address from one of the newspaper articles that had mentioned it. Furthermore, he began toying with the notion of creating a public persona for himself—an anonymous identity that law enforcement and the public could use to refer to him. The idea was not yet fully realized, but he signed two of his letters with the unique symbol that looked like a cross between the number 3 and the letter Z.

After mailing the letters so they were postmarked on the six-month anniversary of Cheri's death, the killer was undoubtedly disappointed when there was no mention of them in the Riverside newspapers. The police department collected the three letters, made some effort to determine who wrote them, chalked up the incident to a prank, and filed them away where they remained until Paul Avery discovered them three years later.

3.4   David Faraday and Betty Lou Jensen December 20, 1968

Interestingly, the Lake Herman Road murders of David Faraday and Betty Lou Jensen were the Zodiac crimes that most precisely aligned with a solstice or equinox. The killer shot David and Betty Lou at approximately 11:15 p.m. on Friday, December 20, 1968, just forty-five minutes before the day of the winter solstice and slightly less than twelve hours prior to the solstice's exact time. Likely, there were two factors contributing to this alignment. The first, quite simply, was chance. We know that the killer was predisposed to striking on weekends, so even the fact that the solstice landed on a Saturday in 1968 involved a bit of happenstance. Of course, the dictates of chance also affected the timing of the killer finding his victims. As a point of reference, it's almost certain that, had it not been for William Crow's impressive instincts, he and his girlfriend would have been the killer's first Bay Area victims, an hour and a half before the murders of David Faraday and Betty Lou Jensen. (See Section 2.1 of *The Zodiac Revisited, Volume 1*)

The second, and more meaningful, factor at work in the timing of the crime may well have been the killer's heightened desire to align the murders with the solstice based on the newness of the idea and his underlying persona. As practicality and other influences caused the killer to compromise the alignment of future crimes and actions, his commitment to achieving precise alignment likely diminished. But with this being the killer's first attempt at aligning the crime, the desire to achieve success was high. Relatedly, the evil from darkness symbolism (see Section 3.2.3.1 of *The Zodiac Revisited, Volume 2*) that the man probably associated with his inaugural Zodiac crime also provided additional motivation to achieve a good alignment.

Four days after the murders of David and Betty, the San Diego Police Department — a jurisdiction 500 miles to the south — communicated with the Solano County Sheriff's Office about a possible connection between the nearly five-year-old Swindle homicides and those at Lake Herman Road. This fact illustrates how rare and recognizable these crimes were in 1960s California. Once again, had it not been for the killer's commitment to never using the same weapon twice, law enforcement would have established the connection almost immediately.

3.4.1   Speculative Evolution

The time between April 1967 and December 1968 was surely eventful for the man who would come to be known as the Zodiac. At some point between these two dates, he likely moved from Southern California to somewhere in the San Francisco Bay Area, accepting a job where he worked weekdays from nine to five. Having derived much satisfaction from taunting Riverside residents through his post-offense writing, the man looked upon his move as an opportunity to begin anew. Understanding that if he committed multiple murders and wrote letters after each, they would indisputably be linked together, he accepted — and perhaps even embraced — this situation and incorporated it into his plan. Instead of operating as he did in Southern California, where he took measures to prevent law enforcement from connecting his crimes, he would take a different tack in the Bay Area, creating an anonymous criminal persona and writing the letters as this alter ego. Unlike his previous crimes, which had satisfying but isolated impacts, his Northern California crimes would build upon each other and thereby amplify his ability to strike fear into the hearts of the people in and around San Francisco.

With his goals falling into place, the man began searching for a concept around which to build his persona. Perhaps wanting the imagery to relate to the city he planned to terrorize, he recalled the villainous Dr. Zodiac from a movie he once saw, *Charlie Chan at Treasure Island*. Not only was the movie set in San Francisco, but it also involved one of the primary Bay Area newspapers, the *San Francisco Chronicle*. Of course, the killer didn't call himself Dr. Zodiac — that would have been too obvious. Instead, drawing upon his knowledge of nautical navigation, he decided to call his alter ego the Zodiac after the celestial concept. Undoubtedly this felt apropos since the younger generation, whom he planned to target, was so caught up in astrology, even though they didn't understand the true meaning of the zodiac.

Satisfied with the idea thus far, the man continued to brainstorm about his new persona and decided to formulate a plan for organizing his murders. Perhaps based on a tidbit of knowledge the killer recalled about Japanese maps basing their compass roses off the Chinese zodiac, or perhaps based on his own awareness of the similarity between the zodiac and the compass rose found on nautical charts, the killer chose to commingle the ideas to form the basis of his methodology. After considering the compass rose and reviewing maps of the San Francisco Bay Area, he elected to center the compass rose on Mount Diablo. This choice was likely satisfying both because the name translates to Devil Mountain and because California cartographers have often used the peak as a reference point. Based on actual alignments — or perhaps simply to make the process more complicated and esoteric — he opted to use a compass rose oriented to magnetic north rather than true north.

Continuing, the killer decided to divide the compass rose into four quadrants, each one centered on a cardinal direction. Crafting the rules that he would impose upon himself, he committed to using a different type of weapon in each quadrant. To begin, he selected the quadrant including San Francisco as the "gun" quadrant. Clearly, he surmised that committing a murder in San Francisco would be more difficult than in other areas. Therefore, he chose the weapon that would be easiest to use — and the one that he was most comfortable with — for this challenging geographic area. He resolved to try to align his crime scenes along the 30° divisions of the compass rose that match the divisions of the zodiac. Certainly, he must have realized that it might not always be possible to achieve exact alignment, but he felt he'd be able to do a reasonably good job. The use of the quadrant's assigned weapon, on the other hand, would be easier to accomplish — at least in theory — and, therefore, was an absolute requirement.

The killer likely felt that everything was falling into place, and that by varying the geographic location of the crimes and changing weapons to satisfy his methodology, he felt confident that he'd get away with his crimes. The one thing that he hadn't addressed was *when* he would strike. He knew that he needed to act often enough to maintain a high level of fear but not so often that he'd compromise his ability to get away with the crimes. Again, he turned to the celestial zodiac for guidance. Understanding that the embodied divisions of the nighttime sky were originally chosen to coincide with the solstices and equinoxes — the four astronomically significant times of the year that were an important part of many ancient cultures — the killer decided to incorporate this component of the zodiac into his methodology by resolving to strike near these times.

In thinking about when to start his newly formulated campaign of terror, the killer thoughtfully settled on the winter solstice — the date in late December that corresponds to the longest night of the year. This height of darkness was the perfect setting for the metaphorical birth of the killer's evil persona. There was a problem though. By this point in time, it was late fall of 1968. In order to start on the winter solstice, he needed to act quickly — sooner than he'd like. But if he didn't act soon, he'd have to wait an entire year for the longest night of the year to return. He decided to move forward with his plan, despite the fact that he was somewhat uncomfortable.

Given the available radial lines in the gun quadrant — the lines he labeled 8, 9, and 10 — the killer started looking for an area where he might find desirable victims — lovestruck couples. (See Sections 3.3 and 3.4 of *The Zodiac Revisited, Volume 2*.) The position 8 radial line extended into San Francisco and was probably not where he wanted to start. Position 9 was a possibility, but position 10 looked more promising because it extended through less populated areas. The killer may well have used a string-based navigational tool such as the one shown in Figure 3.2 to find his areas of interest. Once he decided to focus on position 10, he calculated the appropriate angle of interest as $10*30° = 300°$. He then added the magnetic north offset, rounded to the nearest degree, and arrived at an angle of $317°$. Searching this location on the map, he came up with possible areas in the vicinity of Benicia and Vallejo, specifically in the proximity of Lake Herman Road.

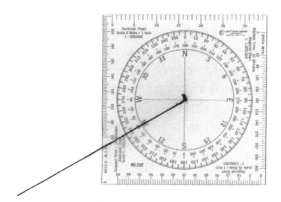

Figure 3.2: An example of a type of string-based navigational tool that the killer may have used when planning his attacks

As he had done with his previous crimes, in early to mid-December, the killer started making trips to his identified area of interest along Lake Herman Road. He may have considered alternate locations along position 10, but ultimately, it was this part of Benicia and Vallejo that he decided would best suit his needs. In fact, he was quite pleased to learn that the general area attracted younger couples hoping to secretly share a few moments of romantic solitude. Various locations along Lake Herman Road resulted in slightly different alignments on the map, but this mattered little. At the proper scale, the alignment was fine. Plus, the process required some flexibility since the man needed to go where victims could be found.

Satisfied with his planning, the man began waiting for the weekend of the winter solstice. In 1968, the solstice fell on Saturday, December 21, so the killer started his mission on Friday evening. If he failed to find acceptable victims that evening, he'd continue on Saturday, but he hoped one of those two nights would yield an acceptable pair of victims since it would be unlikely that he'd easily find the type of couple he was looking for on other nights.

With the arrival of Friday, December 20, the man finished work, quietly had dinner, and headed out to the stretch of Lake Herman Road that he'd previously identified. With his loaded .22-caliber weapon at the ready, he drove back and forth on Lake Herman Road looking for victims of opportunity that matched his desired profile. Just before 10:00 p.m., he drove past the entrance to the Benicia Pumping Station and noticed a young man and woman in a sports car: William Crow and his girlfriend. By the time he realized they were the exact type of victim he was looking for, he had already passed the entrance, so he stopped his car and made a three-point turn. Crow immediately got a bad feeling about the situation; he put his girlfriend's car into gear and quickly left. The killer gave chase, mostly out of frustration, but he soon realized that he'd lost his opportunity.

A little more than an hour later, the killer noticed a station wagon parked in the same spot. Perhaps he drove past David Faraday and Betty Lou Jensen one or more times to confirm his victim profile and then waited for the right moment to strike. Having learned from his earlier experience, he did not abruptly stop and turn around in direct view of the couple. Rather he passed them and, once out of sight, turned around. Convinced that the timing was right, the killer again approached the Benicia Pumping Station and pulled in to the right of David's station wagon. Unsure of what to make of the man, the young couple locked the doors of the station wagon. When he was sure the coast was clear, the man exited his vehicle and fired a single shot into the rear of David's car. He then instructed the young couple to exit the car through the passenger's-side door, probably threatening to kill the couple if they did not comply. Scared and overwhelmed, Betty unlocked her door and the young couple acquiesced. Once the two high school students were standing outside the vehicle, the killer wasted no time shooting David in the head from point-blank range. Doubtless in a state of shock, Betty ran for her life. The killer then turned his attention to the young woman and shot her five times. Satisfied that his two victims had been fatally wounded, the man quickly retreated to his vehicle and left the scene.

Returning to his residence somewhere in the Bay Area, the man savored the aftermath of his crime. As a psychopath, he felt no remorse for the innocent young lives that he so arbitrarily ended. Instead, a morbid sense of excitement likely consumed him as an overwhelming feeling of power coursed through his veins. After the intensity of the evening's events started to fade, the killer began to reflect on the bigger picture of his plan. He'd been forced to act sooner than he wanted to in order to synchronize the emergence of his persona with the winter solstice. Despite the false start he had with the first couple who drove away, everything seemed to go as planned. However, he was still unsure how to incorporate letter writing into his scheme. He wanted to integrate some sort of twist to intensify the impact; he just wasn't sure what that would be. At this point, the important thing was that these murders occurred when they did. He figured he could work out the details of the letter writing later. In fact, he might have preferred to delay his letter writing campaign because, after a second attack, the severity of the threat would be clear. The authorities would understand the seriousness of the situation and, therefore, would not dismiss any attempts at communication, as had happened with the phone calls and six-month anniversary notes in Riverside.

In the days that followed, the killer tracked news of the Lake Herman Road murders in the *Chronicle* and the *Examiner*. He certainly noted that the former put the story on page 10, while the latter gave the news front-page coverage, a day earlier.[11,12] Both papers followed up with additional stories. A few times, he may have ventured out to obtain copies of the *Vallejo Times-Herald*, which covered the murder investigation in more detail. He read that police had learned of his failed encounter with the young couple in the sports car. Furthermore, investigators were considering the possibility that they were dealing with a "murderous maniac."[13] As had been the case in San Diego, where law enforcement used labels such as "psychopathic killer" and "sweetheart slayer," the sheriff's office quickly began to understand the nature of the threat they were up against. Surely, if and when he struck again, this line of reasoning would be reinforced. However, unlike San Diego, the developing perception of his most recent crime vis à vis his persona was precisely what he'd been hoping to achieve this time around. So, rather than feeling troubled, he was pleased with the initial progress.

The man continued to bask in the satisfaction of his sadistic accomplishments, all the while showing up at his job and performing his duties — whatever those may have been — in a way that did not call attention to himself. Meanwhile, time ticked by as it always does. Winter faded away, and before the killer knew it, the spring equinox was upon him. According to his methodology, he should've struck again. However, in December he'd been forced to act before he was ready, and at this point, he was not in a position to strike again. Between the Gaviota and San Diego murders, he had waited eight months. Riverside was two years and nine months after that. Finally, for his first murder as the Zodiac, he'd taken two years and two months to act. So three months was fast — too fast. The man had gotten away with his crimes, thus far, because he'd spent considerable time planning them; hastily perpetrating a crime might have landed him in the custody of law enforcement, and then whatever grand plans he'd had for his persona would matter little. The important point had been to have the Zodiac emerge on the winter solstice; he had done that. Besides, he still hadn't exactly figured out what his first Bay Area letter would look like or to whom it would be sent. He most definitely preferred the *Chronicle* because it had a larger readership, but the *Examiner* was nearly as big and its coverage of his initial crime had been more prominent.

Perhaps during this time he sought some potential attack sites and even made half-hearted attempts at finding victims. But ultimately, the killer decided to let the spring equinox quietly come and go. In the grand scheme of things, this was the best decision. But it was a decision that was not without consequence. The man came to understand and accept that, if he wanted to commit murders at an accelerated pace, he needed to improve his planning — and not just with regard to the next crime. He likely felt that three months was not enough time to conceive of the murder, research it, find an accommodating geographic location, resolve any premeditated situational control, and establish the details of escaping, not to mention communicating with the public. He also needed to ponder venturing outside the gun quadrant, which meant the commission of the crime would become even more difficult.

He may have had some partially formed ideas in terms of the future crimes that he wanted to commit, but with newfound resolve, the killer set out to formulate detailed plans. For his next crime, he decided to focus on another quadrant. Since he wanted authorities to easily associate this crime with his previous one, he directed his attention to the adjacent quadrant, specifically position 11. As you may recall, the Lake Herman Road murders took place along position 10 in the gun quadrant. He labeled this next quadrant "by knife" and began researching locations along position 11, considering premeditated situational control and other related details. Feeling satisfied with the progress, he tentatively scheduled this crime for the summer solstice.

At the same, it's likely that the killer started contemplating another crime, a crime that surely gave the killer a tremendous amount of perverse excitement: striking in the city of San Francisco. By design, the city is located in the gun quadrant, so that aspect required little thought. The city itself is situated along position 8, so the killer began looking at locations along the position 8 radial line. In this particular instance, the crime was is going to be tricky; it was a far cry from lightly traveled Lake Herman Road on the outskirts of Vallejo. Just as important as the perpetration of the crime itself was the concern of successfully escaping from the crime scene. The killer noted that the position 8 radial line intersects the edge of the Presidio Army post, so this could be used to his advantage.

Maybe it was at this point that the man recalled something he saw on television. In 1967, author David Kahn published a book titled *The Codebreakers*, and the promotion of the book included a significant amount of television exposure.* Perhaps witnessing such an appearance inspired the Zodiac to incorporate some form of cryptography into his letters. The killer likely assumed — and rightly so — that if he announced his existence through a letter that included a cipher, people would pay attention. He could then demand that they publish the cipher, just as he had demanded that the Riverside *Press–Enterprise* publish The Confession. The thought of thousands of people slaving over a cipher in the futile hope of discovering his identity undoubtedly filled the man with a perverse, but familiar, satisfaction.

3.5   Mike Mageau and Darlene Ferrin | July 4, 1969

Before the commission of this crime, the killer had murdered seven people across four attacks. There had been no survivors, but that streak came to an end in the Blue Rock Springs parking lot when Mike Mageau lived to tell his story. Ironically, the first time the killer opted to use a larger-caliber weapon (in this case 9 mm) was also the first time a victim's wounds proved nonfatal.

As mentioned previously, stranger murders are inherently difficult to solve. However, the particular people who are murdered can have a significant impact on the resulting investigation. Relatedly, it's difficult to overstate the impact that Darlene Ferrin had on the case of the Zodiac. As an amiable, sociable, and attractive young woman who worked as a waitress, interacting with new people every day, Darlene had a plethora of relationships in her life. To the detriment of the case, these relationships proved to be an ever-fertile source of red herrings.

---

*David Kahn was a member of the American Cryptogram Association — the same organization whose president, Dr. D. C. B. Marsh, authenticated Donald and Bettye Harden's solution of the 408 cipher and challenged the Zodiac to construct a cipher that included his actual name. The association's newsletter from this time frame noted that members had commented on seeing some of Kahn's multiple television appearances.

3.5.1 Speculative Evolution

As the 1969 summer solstice approached, the killer had a lot of loose ends to tie up. Certainly, he'd been giving some thought to the cipher he was planning to send to the newspaper. He knew that he wanted to declare how much he loved killing people — that should sufficiently scare everyone. He also wanted to somehow make reference to the movie *The Most Dangerous Game*. The duality of the hunter (him) being hunted (by law enforcement) seemed apropos. Plus, he remembered the gist of Rainsford's lines about both sides respecting each other during the hunt. He definitely wanted the police to know that they were engaging a worthy opponent.

During this time, the man likely made progress on planning his knife quadrant killing. Many of the areas along the position 11 radial line were not very accommodating in terms of finding couples in an isolated area to perpetrate his crime. However, position 11 passed through the Monticello Dam at the base of Lake Berryessa, so he decided that anything along the water's edge would be fair game. This area had the potential to provide an acceptable level of isolation and, undoubtedly, the opportunity to find couples enjoying each other's company.

At some point, the man reflected on his experience in Gaviota, which had not gone according to plan. This time around, he wanted to perpetrate the crime as he originally intended it: tie up the victims and then stab them. However, based on this previous experience, he realized there was an inherent risk that he could lose control. In the worst case, his victims could even escape. He concluded that he needed a disguise to hide his face from his victims.

During the weekends of June 21–22 and June 28–29, 1969, the killer ventured to Lake Berryessa or possibly to alternative locations along the position 11 radial line. Perhaps he did this prior to concealing his identity and felt uncomfortable perpetrating the crime without a disguise. Perhaps he simply didn't find the type of victims he was looking for. Perhaps he was not in the proper state of mind to execute his higher-level plan. Ultimately, we don't know what happened; we only know that he did not act.

Likely, by the week preceding the fourth of July, the killer was growing increasingly distressed about the situation. He had not acted on the weekend of the summer solstice, nor on the following weekend. He had already let the spring equinox come and go, so he felt the need to do *something*. After considering his options, he elected to defer the attack in the knife quadrant until the fall equinox, which gave him some time to work out whatever problems he was facing. For the summer, he'd return to what worked for him the last time around; he'd go back to the Benicia-Vallejo area and look for another couple. Since this was back in the gun quadrant the crime would be relatively straightforward.

In some ways, he may have reasoned that this was a good idea in its own right. By focusing these first two attacks under the persona of the Zodiac in the same general area, the two crimes would intensify each other, which would not be the case if the second crime was committed elsewhere. By this point, he had already resolved to send his initial Zodiac letter to both the *Chronicle* and the *Examiner*. But by focusing these first two Zodiac crimes around Vallejo, he decided to include the *Vallejo Times-Herald* also.

With the additional months of planning, he also decided to taunt police with a telephone call immediately following the murders. In Riverside, he had called after the fact and had not been taken seriously. But if he called while the police were still reacting to his crime, still trying to piece together exactly what happened, they'd be more likely to pay attention. Moreover, since the details of the crime would not be common knowledge at the time of the call, law enforcement wouldn't dismiss the call as a prank, as had been the case in Riverside. With this strategy in mind, the killer decided to seek out a pay phone in close proximity to the police station. After he resolved to commit his second crime in or near Vallejo, he quietly located a phone booth.

On the night of Friday, July 4, 1969, the killer headed to this now-familiar area near the Vallejo-Benicia border with a plan to strike either that night or the following night. While cruising the extended areas in and around Lake Herman Road, he spotted Darlene Ferrin's car in the Blue Rock Springs parking lot. He parked behind her car to verify that its occupants matched his desired profile and see how they'd react. He noticed a young couple inside the car, and they didn't drive off. Convinced that this was the opportunity he'd been looking for, the killer left the parking lot and drove in the direction from which traffic was most likely to come. By doing this, he could be reasonably sure there'd be no witnesses, at least from one direction. After traveling a couple miles or so, he turned around and drove back toward the parking lot. Unfortunately for Darlene and Mike, the man encountered no one on his way back to them, so he pulled into the parking lot and shot them each several times. (For more details, see Section 2.2 of *The Zodiac Revisited, Volume 1.*)

After the crime, he left the parking lot at a high rate of speed, but soon after, he slowed down and drove in a deliberate manner that would not attract attention. The man proceeded to his predesignated telephone booth, where he called the operator and asked for the Vallejo Police Department. The operator requested the telephone number from where he was calling. Despite refusing to provide the number, he was connected to the VPD. After Nancy Slover recited her standard salutation, the killer delivered the short statement he'd prepared. When Nancy tried to interrupt to ask clarifying questions, he did not let her. Finally, he said "Good-bye" in an unnerving and tauntingly long and drawn-out fashion. Satisfied, he hung up the phone and walked away. As the killer later recounted, the operator performed a "ring back" at the request of the VPD. This surprised the perpetrator and attracted the attention of a passerby. Undeterred, the killer got in his vehicle and headed home.

As had been the case just over six months earlier, the killer closely followed the news of his murderous exploits. In addition to reading the *Chronicle* and the *Examiner*, he obtained copies of the *Vallejo Times-Herald* on Saturday and Sunday and was surprised to learn that Mike Mageau had survived. It is almost certain that he did not read the *Times-Herald* after this, so he did not know that Mageau gave police a physical description of him and his car. This would explain why, in his August 4 letter, the killer assumed that the source of the description must have been the person who saw him near the phone booth on the night of the crime.

Just as the media frenzy from the Blue Rock Springs attack began to fade, the killer turned his attention to letter writing. He'd carefully and thoughtfully constructed his serial-killer persona, the Zodiac, possibly for more than a year. He'd chosen a symbol to represent his alter ego, ⊕, which was significant on multiple levels. He even had his well-branded introductory phrase "This is the Zodiac speaking" worked out and ready for use. However, understanding the value of timing and the subtleties of delivering a message, he decided to hold back his persona's name and the provocative introduction and opted only to use the symbol to sign the first three letters, which he mailed simultaneously.

The most pressing matter, however, was that the Zodiac needed to create the pièce de résistance of his inaugural communication: the cipher. He decided that each of the three newspapers would get one part of the cipher. The individual parts would look and feel similar, with the same number of symbols across the same number of rows and columns, but each paper would not know whether its third of the cipher belonged in position one, two, or three. A would-be decipherer would need to determine which letters corresponded to which symbols, and then arrange the different sections of the cipher in the correct order.

With this goal in mind, the killer began construction of the three-part cryptogram. He gave himself until August 1 to get the cipher and letters done. Playing around with the ideas he envisioned for the content — his general ode to murder and the reference to *The Most Dangerous Game* — he decided to create a cipher with 408 symbols split into three parts, each one comprised of eight rows and seventeen columns.

In addition to recognizing how his communication would satisfy his need for attention, the killer almost certainly considered the practical aspect of the communiqué. There was a real probability that, before all was said and done, the man would end up in the custody of law enforcement. Regardless of the luck he'd had in the past, he planned to commit several more murders throughout the Bay Area. He knew that he could plan and execute his remaining crimes exceptionally well but still end up getting caught. Considering this reality, the killer decided to hedge his bets by suggesting an element of mental illness in his writing, including the idea that he believed his victims would become his slaves in the afterlife. If he ever got caught, he could claim, probably through his legal representation, that the writing indicated he was delusional and disassociated from reality and, therefore, not responsible for his actions. Whether or not this type of argument would have been successful in court is irrelevant. All that matters is that the killer *thought* it could have been successful.

During July, the killer made significant progress on his cipher. For many, but not all of the symbols, he used a sequential assignment approach (see Section 5.2.2 of *The Zodiac Revisited, Volume 2*) in order to cycle through the available symbol choices. When he was at approximately the two-thirds point, the killer took what is likely a substantial break. The cipher sat, partially done.

It's interesting to note that while the killer was exploring the depths of human depravity, other members of our society were, quite literally, expanding the heights of human accomplishment. Between the Blue Rock Springs attack and the date on which the killer mailed his initial Zodiac letters, Neil Armstrong and Buzz Aldrin walked on the moon, and they, along with astronaut Michael Collins, returned safely to Earth, splashing down in the Pacific Ocean.*

Finally, motivated by the impending, self-imposed deadline of August 1, the man resumed the task. In the haste that accompanied his newfound sense of urgency, the killer strayed from the systematic approach he had previously employed. Of particular note, he inadvertently omitted the word "people" while transitioning from the second to the third part of the cipher. Because of this mistake, the

---

*The Apollo 11 mission launched on July 16, 1970. Four days later the crew orchestrated the lunar landing. The mission ended with their return to Earth on July 26.

length of his cipher content reduced from 396 symbols instances — which would have ended five symbol instances into the last row — to 390 symbol instances, leaving more than an entire row of filler.[†] Additionally, he abandoned the meticulous sequential assignment he'd been using. Perhaps he lost track of where he was in terms of cycling through the various homophones.[‡] What we can say is that, for the last third of the cipher, the Zodiac mostly chose symbols from the available options at random. Once he completed the encryption of the cipher content, the killer filled in the remaining eighteen symbols and finished the cipher.

In addition to the three-part cipher, the killer also focused on the accompanying letters. Using the same approach he employed with the six-month anniversary notes a little over two years prior, the man adjusted the same basic content depending on the recipient, changing the names of the other newspapers where appropriate. He also provided several details regarding the Lake Herman Road and Blue Rock Springs attacks to prove that he was, indeed, the killer. He explained the cipher, demanded front-page coverage by August 1, and threatened additional violence if the papers did not comply.

There's a strong probability that the letters were written before the cipher was finished. With the August 1 deadline already written into the letters, this scenario may explain the hasty completion of the cipher and the impossibly small window the killer gave the newspapers to comply with his demands. Whatever the situation, the killer put the final touches on the three-part announcement of his menacing persona and stuffed the letters and ciphers into their corresponding envelopes. Having learned from his experience with The Confession, the man played it safe and affixed twice the necessary postage to the communiqués destined for San Francisco and four times the requisite postage to the envelope going to Vallejo. The killer then dropped

---

[†]You may recall from Section 5.2.2 of *The Zodiac Revisited, Volume 2* that the full 408 symbols instances of the cipher include the content of the cipher and a small number of filler symbols instances after the content.

[‡]Homophones are the name given to different symbols that represent the same letter.

the envelopes into a San Francisco mailbox and, in doing so, introduced a unique collection of letters into the annals of criminal-justice history.

In the days that followed the mailing of the letters, the killer likely acted much as he did in the aftermath of the murders, paying close attention to stories about his communication on television, radio, and in the *Chronicle* and *Examiner*. At his convenience, perhaps over the weekend, he ventured out to get copies of the *Vallejo Times-Herald*. However, he was not pleased with the coverage. Only the *Examiner* published a story on August 1, and that article appeared on page 3 and omitted the cipher. The other two newspapers followed suit on Saturday, August 2. Finally, on Sunday, the joint edition of the *Chronicle* and *Examiner* printed an article that reproduced all three parts of the cipher. In a turn of events that certainly annoyed the killer, none of the stories appeared on the front page. Unsurprisingly, the killer did not make good on his threat of further violence despite the fact that the newspapers did not fully comply with his wishes, a fact that the Sunday article, "Vallejo Mass Murder Threat Fails" made sure to point out.

3.6 Bryan Hartnell and Cecelia Sheppard September 27, 1969

On September 27, 1969, three female students from Pacific Union College almost certainly encountered the Zodiac. Unbeknownst to them, they were likely saved by a combination of factors. First, but not foremost, they were an imperfect match for the killer's desired victim profile. As discussed, the profile hierarchy was couples, females, and others. Attacking multiple females may well have been more desirable to the killer than attacking a lone female; however, it was still an inferior option compared to attacking a lovestruck couple. But the more important issue, from the killer's perspective, would have been the number of victims. With three women, there would have been a real possibility that one of them could have escaped if the man somehow lost control of the situation. Having lost control in Gaviota and knowing that his disguise would provide relatively limited vision, he likely concluded it was not worth the risk. This was especially true given that his methodology dictated the attacks be committed by knife. If he lost control and ended up shooting the victims, as had happened in Gaviota, the outcome would have been unacceptable to the killer. There's little doubt that the man considered attacking these young women, but given the above factors, he ultimately decided to seek out a more accommodating scenario.

3.6.1   Speculative Evolution

The summer solstice murder had happened neither as easily nor as timely as the killer had hoped, but it was done. More importantly, the man had introduced the world to the Zodiac through letter writing and a cipher that had worked exceptionally well. Perhaps the cipher had been solved a bit more quickly than the killer had anticipated, but that mattered little. The plan had been for somebody to solve the cipher, and the timing worked out fine. Moreover, despite these developments, law enforcement had made scant progress. All in all, the killer found much to like about his situation.

He then turned his attention to the fall equinox, which in 1969 landed on Tuesday, September 23. Determined to strike along position 11 in the knife quadrant, the killer again focused his efforts on Lake Berryessa and finalized his plan. He carefully and meticulously sewed a Zodiac symbol on the chest area of the executioner-style hood that would disguise his identity and strike fear into the hearts of his victims. At the same time, he mentally reviewed the details of his premeditated situational control, complete with the idea of referencing Montana's Deer Lodge Prison to enhance his credibility. The man organized his instruments of murder, including a pistol to control the situation, precut lengths of clothesline, and the primary focus of the attack — a knife. The killer also identified the phone booth from which he'd make his telephone call in the aftermath of the crime. Last, but not least, he secured one or more felt-tip pens. With all of the pieces in place, he waited.

On the Saturday following the fall equinox, the killer left his residence in the Bay Area for the shores of Lake Berryessa. Once there, he began his long and arduous search for victims matching his desired profile. Well into the day, he spotted the three young women whom he seriously considered attacking. But, in the end, he decided against it. By 6:00 p.m., the killer knew time was running out because once the sun set, he'd be unable to effectively manipulate a couple in the way that his crime required. Around this time, he noticed Bryan Hartnell's Karmann Ghia parked along Knoxville Road. The killer parked behind the vehicle and set out to find its occupants, murder kit in hand.

During the next thirty minutes, the killer attacked Bryan Hartnell and Cecelia Shepard, who had the clichéd misfortune of being in the wrong place at the wrong time. (See Section 3.1 of *The Zodiac Revisited, Volume 1* for details of this attack.) Shortly after the attack, the killer used his black felt-tip pen to draw his Zodiac symbol and write the dates of his two previous attacks on Bryan's car. Wanting to make certain everyone involved understood the timing of the attack relative to the soon-to-be-placed telephone call, the killer made a point to note the time.

Satisfied with the message on Bryan's car, the killer returned to his vehicle and made his way to the Napa telephone booth he'd picked out in advance. Upon arriving, the man called the Napa Police Department. Learning from his previous experience, the killer simply set the handset down after making his statement, thus preventing the operator from initiating a ring back. He climbed back into his vehicle and returned to his residence somewhere in the San Francisco Bay Area.

3.7   Paul Stine | October 11, 1969

The murder of Paul Stine is remarkable for a variety of reasons. Not only did the killer violate the patterns evident in his previous timing and victim selection, he also struck for the first time within the city limits of San Francisco, created a new identity verification mechanism through the use of Paul's bloodstained shirt, and heightened the level of public terrorism by threatening to kill schoolchildren. Indeed, killing Paul Stine and sending a letter to the *Chronicle* in the days following the murder were the two most impactful actions in the entirety of the Zodiac's existence. In hindsight, these two actions precipitated the public hysteria that reached its height in mid-October 1969.

From this perspective, we can look at the ends as a way of explaining the means. Had the killer not murdered Paul Stine *in San Francisco*, his impact would have been diminished. Had the Zodiac not broken his pattern of targeting couples, his impact would have been diminished. Had he not killed Paul Stine just two weeks after his previous murder, his impact would have been diminished. And, of course, had the man not threatened schoolchildren, his impact would have been greatly diminished. All of these factors came together, reinforced each other, and served to support the tremendous level of impact that the Zodiac achieved. Each one was a necessary element.

Another observation we can make regarding the murder of Paul Stine relates to the specific location in Presidio Heights. We know that the killer requested a destination of Washington and Maple Streets. For reasons unknown, he directed Paul to drive one additional block, to Washington and Cherry, whereupon he killed the cab driver and then calmly left the scene of the crime, walking north on Cherry and turning east on Jackson — where he encountered SFPD Officers Donald Fouke and Eric Zelms — before entering the Presidio. Clearly, the killer chose this location for its close proximity to the large, wooded area of the Presidio, which he used to facilitate his escape. However, we also have to keep in mind that he arrived at the location via Paul Stine's taxicab and, therefore, could have given any destination within Presidio Heights. In particular, if his only desire was to commit the crime and get away undetected, he could have given a destination along Jackson, thus avoiding the need to walk one block north. Furthermore, in this area of Presidio Heights, Jackson is the last street that runs parallel to the park before the entrance. However, Cherry and Maple both extend slightly past Jackson before they dead-end. If he had directed Paul to pull into one of these areas, it would have been considerably easier for the killer to commit the crime and escape unnoticed. However, he did none of this.

The conclusion that I am compelled to draw from these circumstances is that the killer *wanted* to have witnesses. He *wanted* one or more people in the Presidio Heights neighborhood to report having seen him. He *wanted* to walk in the open for some distance, before disappearing into the Presidio. In fact, it's possible that the killer instructed Stine to drive the additional block in order to *increase* the likelihood of being seen, either by way of lengthening the distance he needed to walk before vanishing into the park or by executing the crime in an area where he was more likely to be seen. From his perspective, residents might call the police, but it was extremely doubtful that witnesses would confront him if they knew or suspected he was armed. What he likely neither wanted nor expected was an encounter with an SFPD patrol car — whatever that encounter may have been. However, he undoubtedly was pleased with the way events unfolded since it provided even more fodder with which to taunt law enforcement.

Continuing this line of reasoning, if he wanted to be seen, then he must have been comfortable with witnesses providing a description of his looks. These thoughts suggest that the killer was being truthful when he claimed to be using some type of disguise. The disguise itself may have been anywhere along the spectrum from simple to sophisticated; we cannot infer much about it. What we can conclude, based on these observations and what else we know about the case, is that people who encountered the man during the pursuit of normal life activities likely did not suspect him to be the Zodiac.

3.7.1 Speculative Evolution

With Lake Berryessa being the first crime he committed after introducing the Zodiac to the world, the killer savored the reaction of the news media, which, at this point, was starting to develop an understanding of the man. Though they generally still referred to him as the "Cipher Killer" instead of the name the man preferred, he worried little. Because the killer had written to both the *Chronicle* and *Examiner* in the wake of the Blue Rock Springs attack, both San Francisco newspapers covered the happenings at Lake Berryessa in more depth. As a result, the killer may have been less inclined to seek out local coverage of his Lake Berryessa attack, especially given the travel distance it likely required. Again, the *Examiner*'s coverage was earlier and more substantial than that of the *Chronicle*.

As discussed in *The Zodiac Revisited, Volume 2*, Section 3.2.3.2, one headline in particular surely attracted the killer's attention. On September 30, 1969, the Zodiac achieved his first Bay Area front-page headline by way of the *Examiner*. The headline was a provocation that asserted "Police Dare Cipher Killer." Without reading the story, it would appear that police were daring the killer to strike again. The reality was more mundane and perhaps a bit too predictable — the Napa County Sheriff's Office was daring the killer to write another letter, this time supplying the portion of the message from Bryan Hartnell's car door* that they were withholding.

Surely, there were a number of different dynamics at work by this point in time. First and foremost, the killer was likely already planning his next crime, which, according to his methodology, would take place on or about the winter solstice. This attack would be his first in San Francisco proper along position 8 — this, of course, became the murder of Paul Stine, albeit not at the time of the winter

---

*The omitted phrase was "by knife."

solstice. Since, by this time, the killer's ultimate goal was to terrorize the people of the Bay Area, moving into the San Francisco city limits was an important step.

As a secondary consideration, the killer had undoubtedly come to understand, either consciously or subconsciously, the concept that I previously described as "murder velocity" in Section 3.2.3.3 of *The Zodiac Revisited, Volume 2*. In other words, if he wanted to achieve an exceptionally high level of impact, at some point he would need to strike more often than once every three months. That rate, while significant and undeniably sure to garner attention, would not overshadow all of the competing issues of the day, including other instances of serial murder such as Charles Manson (also in California) and Michigan's John Norman Collins. Again, as alluded to in the discussion of methodology, the killer did not consider acting in addition to the solstices and equinoxes a violation of his self-imposed rules. On the contrary, he was open to augmenting his methodology.

At this point, the desired victim profile was another factor affecting the killer's actions. The murder of Paul Stine was a turning point because it marked the moment in time when the Zodiac switched from being primarily concerned about the means of his actions to being mostly concerned about their ends. Prior to October 11, 1969, the killer was constructing a context to terrorize the people of the Bay Area; however, his primary message was in the means of his terrorism. By murdering young, lovestruck couples in romantic environments, he was communicating the fundamental grievance that had motivated him to kill. He was socially dysfunctional, especially with members of the opposite sex. In response to the resultant frustration, he had developed a profound hatred of women and a psychopathic jealousy of the couples who were able to achieve the meaningful, intimate relationships that he himself could not. However, when he planned Paul Stine's murder, this element of his message was nowhere to be found. Instead, killing Stine was all about the strategic value it provided to the task of terrorizing the Bay Area and, to a lesser degree, satisfying the geographic component of his methodology.

In response to seeing his first Bay Area headline, the killer surely reacted with perverse excitement and resolved to accept law enforcement's "dare," albeit on his own terms. He decided not to write and provide the omitted phrase as requested — that would have been too cooperative. Rather, he accelerated his plan of striking within the borders of San Francisco. The killer rescheduled the crime that had been tentatively planned for the winter solstice — the one-year anniversary of the Zodiac's emergence — to be carried out as soon as possible. Not only would this new course of action serve as a resounding response to law enforcement's so-called dare, but by striking so soon after his previous murder at Lake Berryessa, the amount of fear generated by the Zodiac's mere presence would be amplified substantially. Each day, the people of the Bay Area would wonder if this was the day that yet another person would die at the hands of the mysterious bogeyman known as the Zodiac. Each evening that the sun set on the Bay Area without the killer being apprehended would be yet another reminder to residents that law enforcement was powerless to stop him.

When he originally devised the plan to attack in San Francisco, the killer may have toyed with the idea of targeting a couple, or alternatively, a lone woman. However, perhaps to increase his persona's terroristic impact, the man realized that changing the victim profile would increase the level of unpredictability which, in turn, would amplify the levels of fear and uncertainty. The dysfunction that had, for so long, motivated the killer to terrorize society was still an important component of his psychological makeup. However, the terrorism itself had evolved to a point where it was a significant consideration in its own right.

Taking these constraints into account along with the requirements of committing a murder in San Francisco and in close proximity to the position 8 radial line, the killer finalized his plan. He would start by parking his car at a location where, after the crime, he could enter the Presidio near Julius Kahn Park, travel on foot through the park, and emerge at an alternate location near the car. Entering the park would create an impossibly large search area which, in turn, would facilitate his escape. After parking his car, he would make his way to Union Square, probably on foot, and then flag down a taxi, requesting a destination at the intersection of Washington and Maple Streets. The Zodiac would murder the cab driver, thereby violating his previously established pattern and increasing his level of unpredictability. After removing a section of the victim's bloodstained clothing, the killer would walk through Presidio Heights — during which time he probably hoped somebody would see him — before finally entering the park and trekking back to his car.

Likely on the weekend preceding Paul Stine's death, the killer made a practice run of his plan, possibly working out some of the final details. On the evening of October 11, he donned some form of disguise that made his physical appearance resemble the composite drawings that would be made in the upcoming days. He drove to his designated vehicle drop-off point and set out to execute his plan with his 9 mm weapon carefully concealed. After arriving at Union Square, the killer flagged down Paul Stine's taxicab and requested a destination of Washington and Maple. At the end of the three-and-a-half mile drive, the killer instructed Paul to continue one block farther, perhaps in an effort to increase the likelihood of being seen. With the moment having arrived, the Zodiac raised his weapon and, with a single bullet, ended Paul's tragically short life. The killer moved to the front seat, quickly and callously removed a section of Paul's bloodstained shirt, pocketed his wallet and keys, wiped down certain areas of the cab, and — probably intentionally — left a partial bloody fingerprint on a section of the doorframe. Inadvertently, or perhaps as an instance of intentional misdirection, the killer left a pair of size 7 leather gloves in the back seat. Satisfied with the state of the cab, the man began to walk north on Cherry Street and casually turned east onto Jackson.

Without knowing that the SFPD received an inaccurate description of the suspect, the killer faced what must have been an unexpected and frightening sight — a patrol car coming straight at him. Though I accept that knowledgeable people have alternative viewpoints, I believe that Officer Zelms spoke to the killer through his rolled-down window and that the Zodiac calmly misdirected the officers similar to the scenario described in the Bus Bomb Letter. Moments later, Officer Fouke drove off and the Zodiac disappeared into the Presidio. After some amount of time in the park—exactly how long is unclear—the killer made his way to his car and headed home.

The next day, the killer sat down and composed the most effectual letter of his entire body of work. Given that he'd finally struck within San Francisco proper, he'd modified his victim selection so that nobody would feel secure, and that this latest crime occurred just two short weeks after the last, the killer threw out one last way to up the ante. He added a threat against society's most defenseless and cherished members: children. The killer knew that nothing is more disturbing to parents than the threat of bodily harm or death to their children. When the public entered a state of panic as a result of his latest threat, law enforcement would undoubtedly come away looking inept and powerless. With these thoughts in mind, the killer completed his letter, added a swatch of Paul Stine's bloodstained shirt, sealed the envelope, and dropped it into a mailbox.

In the weeks following the Stine Letter, the media coverage surrounding the Zodiac case reached its pinnacle. The public was inundated with Zodiac-related stories on television, radio, and in the print media. Knowledge of the killer transcended the boundaries of the Bay Area as national news organizations took an interest in his exploits. People across the country were morbidly fascinated by the cold-blooded killer who communicated with the people he terrorized through cryptic, handwritten letters; a murderer who challenged the intellects of all those who dared to try solving his ciphers; a madman who violated society's unspoken rule of never threatening innocent, defenseless children. Never before and never again would the killer command such attention.

By the time the Sam episode played out (see Section 3.3 of *The Zodiac Revisited, Volume 1*), the media had subjected the citizens of the Bay Area to a constant and relentless barrage of Zodiac coverage. When the winter solstice rolled around, the killer had plenty on his mind. First and foremost, he'd already perpetrated the attack that he'd earmarked for the celestial event, that had become Paul Stine's murder. Second, he'd been so consumed with other Zodiac-related activities — such as crafting and sending the 340 cipher, responding to Martin Lee's unflattering characterizations, and conceiving of and communicating the bus bomb threat — that he likely wasn't fully prepared to perpetrate another crime. Again, despite his psychopathy, the man was very disciplined. Third, the close encounter with Officers Fouke and Zelms after the Stine murder may have played a role in his decision to lay low for a while.

As he had done in the spring, the killer let the winter solstice pass without perpetrating a crime. Like a person on an exercise regiment whose exuberance results in doing more than planned, the killer was still on a high from his previous murder, so he rationalized away the need to stick to the original schedule. Also, because the killer was prolifically writing letters to the people of the Bay Area at this point, he had another activity to fulfill his need for attention. However, he was still determined to commemorate the winter solstice in some manner, so he decided to send a special letter to Melvin Belli, whom he came to view in a positive light following the flamboyant attorney's appearance on *A.M. San Francisco*. Because letter writing afforded the killer the opportunity to precisely control the timing of his actions, he mailed the communiqué so that it would be postmarked on the anniversary of the Lake Herman Road murders.

3.8 Kathleen Johns | March 22, 1970

Many works on the Zodiac,[3,14,15] especially early ones, unquestionably regard the man as Kathleen Johns's abductor. Kathleen's identification of the fugitive from the composite drawing she saw coupled with the killer's subsequent claim of responsibility seemed to paint the appropriate picture.

However, as time passed and the investigation continued to stagnate, seeds of doubt began to germinate. Subscribers to the increasingly popular Taking Credit theory viewed apparent inconsistencies in Kathleen's recounting of events as evidence of dishonesty — both on her part and the Zodiac's. As explained in Section 1.3.4 of *The Zodiac Revisited, Volume 2*, this flawed belief even made it into the script of David Fincher's movie *Zodiac*.

Principal among the alleged issues of credibility is the apparent discrepancy between the undramatic way in which Kathleen described events at the time of the incident — based on police reports and the two known newspaper articles — and the significantly more dramatic version she later recounted as exemplified in Robert Graysmith's book *Zodiac*. For example, this discrepancy can be seen in the juxtaposition of her reported conversations with the killer. One of the original police reports stated:

> *Complainant stated the suspect was quite friendly with her, did not make any advances toward her, or threats toward her, and when asked if he was going to stop he would merely elude the question and start talking about something else.*[16]

Similarly, the *Examiner* reported:

> *At no time did the man make any advances toward her, but he rambled on — despite her pleas to find a garage.*[17]

In the later, more dramatic version of the story,* Kathleen claimed the man kept repeating the statements "You know you're going to die," and "You know I'm going to kill you."

The other major difference between the two versions of the story has to do with how the man reacted when Kathleen bolted from the

---

*This more dramatic version was popularized by Robert Graysmith's book, which was published sixteen years after the incident. However, Kathleen reported the same dramatic version of events in an interview with Paul Avery just eight months after the abduction.[3]

car — with her infant daughter in her arms — and hid. The police reports and the initial articles related that the man did little more than close the passenger's-side door and drive away. However, Kathleen later claimed that the man exited his vehicle and started searching for her with a flashlight, abandoning the task only when confronted by a truck driver who stopped and asked what was going on.

Sadly, Kathleen Johns passed away in 2002 — yet another person directly impacted by the deeds of the Zodiac who ultimately left this world without the satisfaction of any resolution.

Given all of this uncertainty, it's understandable that people question Kathleen's credibility, which, in turn, casts doubt on the credibility of the Zodiac, and therefore, potentially bolsters the case for the Taking Credit theory. But a deeper consideration of all available facts suggests that this is not the correct way to view the Kathleen Johns incident. Rather, the kidnapping of Kathleen and her infant daughter along with the subsequent torching of her vehicle more closely align with the original perception of the crimes — in other words, that the Zodiac was, indeed, responsible. As a consequence, the related support for the Taking Credit theory diminishes, and the probability that the killer was being truthful in his communications increases.

The first point to consider when trying to untangle the inconsistencies surrounding this curious incident is that the reporters who wrote the previously mentioned articles in the *Modesto Bee* and the *Examiner* did not interview Kathleen Johns. Their content was clearly derived from the police reports and was possibly augmented with clarifications from the police officers who took her statement. Therefore, agreement between the police reports and these newspaper articles is a moot point that in no way represents independent corroboration.

Second, in a lengthy 1998 interview, Kathleen elaborated on her interactions with the Patterson Police Department in the hours following her ordeal.[18] Of particular note, she described that the officer on duty took the initial part of her statement — the time during which the abductor was relatively nonthreatening toward her. But once she spotted the composite sketch of the Zodiac and asserted that *he* was her abductor, the officer discontinued the formal recording of her statement. At that point, Kathleen claimed the officer abandoned her and her infant daughter in an empty and darkened diner, where he instructed her to wait until further notice. Feeling like she had little choice, she and her daughter waited for what turned out to be hours. When queried about the fate of the police report, Kathleen explained: "The report I gave is the report I had given up to that point."

When the police finally returned to Kathleen and her daughter, they were transported to the San Joaquin County Sheriff's Office. Kathleen acknowledged retelling her story to law enforcement personnel at that office. However, at that point, given that she was six hours away from home, she had likely been abducted by a serial killer, and she had been left alone by police for hours without food or supplies for her infant daughter, it's not surprising that there was some tension between her and law enforcement. Therefore, it's easy to imagine that her willingness to cooperate may have reached its limit.

Third, as a result of Paul Avery's interview of Kathleen Johns, the *Chronicle* published the more dramatic version of events eight months after the incident as part of an article that introduced the possible connection between the Zodiac and the murder of Cheri Jo Bates.[3] This interview may have been the first time Kathleen publicly recounted the full details of her ordeal. Moreover, Kathleen's subsequent retellings of the events varied relatively little from this version.

A fourth consideration that has remained unappreciated for much of its existence is the timing of the incident. Kathleen's ordeal began on the evening of Sunday, March 22, 1970. The spring equinox occurred on Friday, March 20 — just two days prior. In other words, the perpetration of this crime on the weekend most closely associated with the spring equinox aligned perfectly with the timing aspect of the Zodiac's methodology.

Finally, the use of sabotage followed by a Good Samaritan ruse, which was present in both the murder of Cheri Jo Bates and the abduction of Kathleen Johns, provides a mutually supportive argument that both women were victims of the same man. The perpetrator's use of the same type of premeditated situational control reinforces all the other evidence that suggests the same man was responsible for both crimes.

*   *   *

Another interesting aspect of this crime is the interaction that centered around Kathleen's ten-month-old daughter, Jennifer. According to Robert Graysmith in his book *Zodiac*, Kathleen Johns said the abductor told her: "I'm going to throw the baby out."[19] However, the precise statement that Kathleen made in her 1998 interview conveyed a subtle, but important, difference. Specifically, she claimed that the abductor kept demanding that *she* "Throw that baby out."[18] In other words, the abductor was not going to throw the baby out, rather, he wanted Kathleen to do it. Unsurprisingly, she refused.

This minor difference in wording is important because it clearly reflects the abductor's perception of the situation. The baby was the problem that was preventing the killer from acting and, thus, causing him to drive around aimlessly, not knowing what to do. He was ready, able, and willing to act in the pursuit of ending Kathleen's young life, but he was unable to bring himself to the point of murdering an innocent infant. The killer had obviously threatened school-age children and had possibly even taken steps to murder or maim them. But apparently, a line in the man's psyche was drawn somewhere between school-age children and infants, and this baby was a problem he was not prepared to handle. His only solution was to demand that the mother throw the baby out the window — a plan that I'm sure even he did not expect to work.

Parents often save the lives of their infant children. Rarely, however, does an infant save the life of a parent. The circumstances under which such an occurrence can happen are simply infrequent. Nevertheless, there is little doubt that in the late evening hours of March 22, 1970, it was the mere presence of ten-month-old Jennifer — who was initially hidden from view — that foiled the plans of a psychopath and, in the process, saved the life of her mother. Kathleen later passed away at the relatively young age of fifty-five, but had it not been for her daughter, she would have died more than thirty years earlier.

3.8.1   Speculative Evolution

Satisfied with the media circus following his recent flurry of activity, sometime around late 1969 or early 1970, the killer stepped back and started planning for the upcoming spring equinox. Having struck three times within the gun quadrant — including, most recently, once within San Francisco — one time in the knife quadrant, and having cryptically suggested in the Bus Bomb Letter that his improvised explosive device was intended for the fire quadrant, the killer turned his attention to the last remaining quadrant.

With the rope quadrant centered around the position 3 radial line, the man began to brainstorm ways to murder his next victim(s). As had been the case with Lake Berryessa, the use of the quadrant's weapon — rope — would be considerably more difficult than a firearm. Therefore, he would, once again, need to employ premeditated situational control to create the requisite circumstances.

The killer began scouting geographic areas in the target quadrant on his map of California. As he had done with his previous murders, he likely began making exploratory trips to various destinations within that quadrant. After considering the difficulty of attacking someone with a rope and taking into account all possible scenarios so he could control the situation, the killer decided to target a lone woman. This choice would also effectively terrorize the people of the Bay Area because it would again emphasize the killer's unpredictability. It was also a practical choice because the killer would have to physically subdue his victim at some point during the perpetration of the crime. Finally, because women bear the brunt of the killer's hatred, he certainly found some degree of satisfaction in his decision.

Returning to the same line of thought that he employed with Cheri Jo Bates — the last time his target was a lone woman — he once again started thinking about how he could entrap an individual female via automotive difficulty. Continuing to understand how easily people can be manipulated when they believe they are being helped, the man decided to employ the same type of premeditated situational control he had used in Riverside, namely sabotage followed by a Good Samaritan ruse. After reviewing the geographic features of his chosen area of attack, the killer combined all the relevant ingredients and formulated the plan of action that we know he employed with Kathleen Johns.

Unlike the times he was targeting couples, which typically involved trying to find victims on a Friday or Saturday, this time the killer opted to carry out his criminal pursuits on a Sunday evening, when Highway 132 was nearly deserted.* In 1970, the spring equinox arrived on Friday, March 20. Two days later, the killer set his plan into action, by driving to Modesto and positioning himself in an area where he could observe traffic entering or passing through on Highway 132. Moreover, he made sure that he could clearly view the occupants of the vehicles because he was targeting an automobile driven by a lone, youthful woman. Sometime around 11:00 p.m., the Zodiac witnessed Kathleen Johns's station wagon drive by after having stopped for gas in Modesto. Convinced that this was the opportunity he'd been waiting for, the man pulled onto the highway and began to follow Kathleen.

What the killer had no way of knowing was that Kathleen's ten-month-old daughter, Jennifer, was asleep in the back of the station wagon, hidden from view. Also unbeknownst to the man, Kathleen was seven months pregnant. All in all, he'd chosen a potential victim who was far from his ideal. Unfortunately for Kathleen, the killer did not realize these circumstances until he was irrevocably committed to his plan.

After Kathleen saved herself and Jennifer by jumping from the killer's car and hiding from him until he was forced to drive away,

---

*An alternative, but less likely, possibility is that the killer made unsuccessful attempts to commit the crime on Friday and/or Saturday night.

the Zodiac returned to the abduction site and torched Kathleen's station wagon, mostly out of frustration. Unlike the false start the killer had with William Crow and his girlfriend on Lake Herman Road, this failed attempt involved felony kidnapping and several threats against the victim's life. Soon, law enforcement would be investigating the incident and likely paying close attention to his chosen stretch of Highway 132. As a result, he would not be able to move on to another victim in the same area using the same MO. He was done for the evening, and, more importantly, the plan, into which the killer had invested considerable time and effort, was no longer viable. Disappointed, the Zodiac was forced to abort his spring equinox activity.

3.9   Officer Richard Radetich | June 19, 1970

In the early morning hours of Friday, June 19, 1970, twenty-five-year-old San Francisco Police Officer Richard Radetich was alone in his patrol car writing a traffic citation when an unknown assailant approached his vehicle and fired three shots through the driver's-side window. Officer Radetich was hit in the left temple. Residents living nearby heard the gunshots and called police. Radetich was rushed to the hospital, but he died that evening.

Law enforcement's initial attempts to glean information from the residents in the proximity of Radetich's murder were minimally successful. Reports indicated that people had seen neither the gunman nor his car. Rather, they had heard the gunshots and, soon after, the sounds of a vehicle speeding away. However, a few blocks away a gas station attendant told police that shortly after the shooting, he saw "a white Cadillac racing east on Oak Street."[20]

There was also little physical evidence at the scene that proved useful. The only meaningful clue was a single 0.38-caliber shell casing found outside the shattered window of Radetich's car. The existence of this shell casing and the specifics of its caliber were reported in the initial *Chronicle* story detailing Officer Radetich's murder.[20]

People who subscribe to the Taking Credit theory view this fact as meaningful data to support their position; in other words, they believe the Zodiac used these details from the *Chronicle* to bolster his claim that he had committed the murder.

When an officer dies in the line of duty, it often strikes an emotional chord in the community. We, as people, understandably tend to live our lives in a way that focuses our attention, first and foremost, on the happenings within our immediate world. For instance, we concentrate on our needs, our goals, and our relationships. We often lose sight of the very real dangers that police officers confront on a daily basis to establish and maintain public safety. But when one of them dies in the line of duty, we not only stop to take note, we also pause and reflect to gain perspective.

In the case of Officer Radetich, the circumstances were especially tragic, which heightened the community's sense of loss. The young SFPD officer was just twenty-five years old. He left behind a wife and an eight-month-old daughter. Everyone who knew him said virtually the same thing: all he ever wanted to do was become a police officer. Adding to the senselessness of the tragedy, Radetich was not killed while performing some high-risk police action, such as the apprehension of a dangerous criminal, rather, he lost his life while sitting in his car writing a ticket.

In fact, at the time of Radetich's death, the SFPD had a security policy in place requiring that there were always two officers per patrol car. Having a single officer in a police car was deemed an unacceptable safety risk. The only exception to this rule was made for patrol cars from the Traffic Division, Officer Radetich's division. The department deemed this division's activity to be lower risk and, therefore, did not enforce the policy. Unsurprisingly, in the wake of Officer Radetich's death, the Chief of Police immediately expanded the policy to apply to *all* patrol cars.[21]

Apart from the general tumultuousness associated with the era, San Francisco was in the midst of a time of heightened violence. One particularly troubling aspect of this violence was an increase in the number of officers killed in the line of duty. Officer Radetich was the third member of the SFPD killed in 1970. The sentiment of many was perhaps best expressed by the person who was in charge of arranging the fallen officer's funeral. "Look — 25 years ago we said we'd give a free funeral to any policeman or fireman killed in the line of duty. Before this year — for, oh, about 17 years, I guess — there were just three or four policemen killed. Then this year, three funerals already. What's happening?"[22] In truth, in the prior seventeen years, thirteen officers had been killed. Regardless, the statement reflected the frustration felt by many.

Interestingly, the Zodiac had a connection, of some sort, with all three officers who were killed in the line of duty during the first six months of 1970. Officer Eric Zelms, who encountered the Zodiac during the manhunt following Paul Stine's murder, was shot by his own service revolver after a citizen wrestled it away from him during an altercation in the early morning hours of January 1, 1970.[23] Brian McDonnell was the second officer killed in the line of duty in 1970. He died as the result of injuries sustained during the February 18 bombing of San Francisco's Park Station Police Department. In the "My Name Is" Letter, the Zodiac explicitly denied culpability in the highly publicized bombing, despite having made bomb threats of his own. Finally, in his writings, the Zodiac appeared to claim responsibility for the murder of Officer Radetich.

It's hard to overstate the emotional impact that Officer Radetich's murder had on the city of San Francisco.* These solemn circumstances had a strange consequence. Neither law enforcement nor the public were willing to entertain the possibility that the Zodiac had actually committed the crime; it was just too much of a morbid accomplishment. The more comfortable alternative was to embrace Chief of Inspectors Martin Lee's "clumsy criminal" narrative — the idea that the Zodiac was an incompetent, lying, opportunist who had just been incredibly lucky — and imagine the killer lazily reading the newspaper and firing off letters with half-baked claims of responsibility.

---

*Officer Radetich was given the honor of lying in state in San Francisco's City Hall rotunda. More than a thousand people paid their respects, including Mayor Joseph Alioto who returned early from an overseas trip to attend.[24]

Three days after Officer Radetich's murder, police identified Joe Allen Johnson as a suspect in the homicide. Johnson was a thirty-year-old black man who'd had prior run-ins with the law and was "well known" to the residents of the neighborhood. When the SFPD named Johnson as a suspect, he was already wanted for felony assault for holding up a Western Union office.[25]

An alleged eyewitness to Radetich's murder identified Johnson as the killer. When shown a picture of Johnson, the witness "swore that that was the man he saw."[26] Both the *Chronicle* and the *Examiner* published Johnson's picture, and a massive manhunt ensued for the fugitive and his blue Camaro.[25,27] Unfortunately, initial attempts to locate Johnson failed.

Most works on the Zodiac end the story of Radetich's murder here, particularly those by people who argue that the killer was not responsible for the officer's death.* However, there's more to the story.

Several months later, in early November, the FBI arrested Johnson in Xenia, Ohio — the state of his birth. He was charged with: (a) interstate flight to avoid prosecution for assault with a deadly weapon on a police officer, (b) armed robbery, and (c) burglary (with the latter two charges stemming from the earlier criminal act). Two SFPD homicide inspectors were dispatched to Ohio, where they took custody of Johnson and escorted him back to California to stand trial.

According to Johnson, he had left California in 1969, and "the first he learned of the police shooting... was when he saw his picture on a wanted poster."[28] On January 9, 1971, approximately two months after apprehending Johnson, the SFPD dropped the murder charge due to a lack of evidence. In the words of Lieutenant Charles Ellis, head of homicide: "Up to now, we have one witness but we need something more, including corroboration. We're not giving up. We've intensified our investigation."[29]

---

*Perhaps because it was a fictionalized account rather than a documentary, the 2007 movie *Zodiac* went a step further and claimed, through the use of dialogue, that "The police already had somebody in custody" at the time of the Zodiac's letter.

Johnson was found guilty on the other charges, but law enforcement was never able to make a case against him for the murder of Officer Radetich. One thing is certain — the murder of a police officer, especially a wanton murder such as that of Officer Radetich, is neither easily forgotten nor lightly pursued. The fact that the charges were dropped due to lack of evidence clearly implies that no additional corroborative evidence could be turned up despite significant efforts. In light of these facts, Johnson's initial reaction to the charges — that he only learned of them after seeing himself on a "wanted" poster — was likely a sincere and accurate reaction.

If the Zodiac was indeed responsible for the murder of Officer Radetich — and I believe he was — it's an interesting sidenote that the killer twice benefited by being mistaken for a black male: first through the inaccurate dispatch immediately following the Stine murder where the suspect was erroneously described as an NMA (negro male adult) and later via the misguided pursuit of Joe Allen Johnson.

It's highly probable that the Zodiac murdered Officer Radetich, just as he implied. The unprovoked, blitz-style attack was consistent with previous homicides he had committed. Also, the timing and location of the murder fit well within the methodology proposed in Chapter 3 of *The Zodiac Revisited, Volume 2*. Law enforcement was unable to locate Joe Allen Johnson in the days following Radetich's murder because he was already back in Ohio by that point, just as he said. The single witness who pointed the finger at Johnson was either mistaken or, more likely, had a more nefarious motive. Either way, corroborating evidence was not found because the described scenario is not what happened. In other words, the initial situation as communicated by the public — that nobody had seen the perpetrator — was likely the truth. Moreover, the killer did not drive a blue Camaro, as Johnson did; instead, he was likely driving the white Cadillac seen speeding away from the scene of the crime.

In a pattern that happened again and again in the extended crimes of the Zodiac: the killer murdered somebody with whom he had absolutely no prior acquaintance, and the investigation floundered due to an incorrect focus on suspects associated with the victim or the crime. This scenario played out with Cheri Jo Bates and the Riverside Police Department's focus on their local suspect. It also happened with Darlene Ferrin, whose tremendous likability and substantial collection of friends created countless red herrings. The phenomenon was again at work when the police focused on a potential suspect named Lawrence Kane, a troubled man who had the misfortune of working in proximity to Donna Lass. The Zodiac's decision to murder strangers and his choice to adhere to a self-imposed methodology in the Bay Area not only complicated some of the relevant investigations, it downright derailed them.

*   *   *

The first and most important aspect of Richard Radetich's murder was its timing. The officer was gunned down in the predawn darkness of Friday, June 19, 1970. The summer solstice occurred just two days later, making this alignment perfect in terms of the proposed methodology. This timing is an important reason why we should take the killer's implied claim of responsibility seriously.

The next consideration, from a methodology perspective, was the location of Officer Radetich's murder. As we saw with the murder of Paul Stine, most of San Francisco lies along or near the position 8 radial line of the rotated compass rose. Again, because position 8 fell within the gun quadrant, the murder of the young officer was consistent with this aspect of the methodology. Figure 3.3 shows the rotated compass rose superimposed over the Bay Area and the Radetich crime-scene location identified.

The final important clue that the Zodiac provided was another instance of spatial information. This clue came from the large Zodiac symbol used to communicate the killer's victim count on page 2 of the *Mikado* Letter, which was mailed just over a month after Radetich's murder. In this instance, the author recorded his score as "13," which, according to his standard taunting mechanism, meant he'd killed thirteen victims. The more interesting part, however, was the recording of the complementary "SFPD = 0." In particular, the

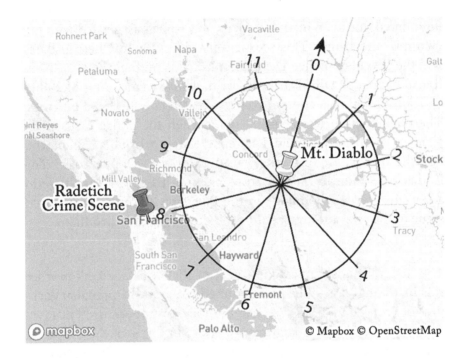

Figure 3.3: The rotated compass rose superimposed over the Bay Area to show the alignment of the Radetich crime scene. The location is generally aligned with position 8 and well within the gun quadrant.

killer had significantly emphasized the zero by going over the circle again and again. Furthermore, the killer wrote this component of the score such that the zero was located near position 8 of the Zodiac symbol — in other words, the position that corresponded to San Francisco on the rotated compass rose. Figure 3.4 again shows the Bay Area, this time with the Zodiac symbol overlaid and rotated to the appropriate 17° of magnetic declination.* The location of the Radetich crime scene is also shown on the map. This figure highlights the symbolism that the killer intended to communicate. In drawing the overemphasized zero, he symbolically circled the

---

*As described in Section 3.3 of *The Zodiac Revisited, Volume 2*, magnetic north in San Francisco during the Zodiac — to the nearest degree — was 17° east (clockwise). On the Phillips 66 map, the Zodiac explained that "0 is to be set to Mag. N."

location of the Radetich crime scene. Last, but not least, the killer identified this location on the Zodiac symbol with "SFPD = 0" instead of some other means such as simply using an *X*, as he had done in the past, because the victim was a *member* of the SFPD. In a symbolic sense, we can read "SFPD = 0" as "SFPD equals this location."

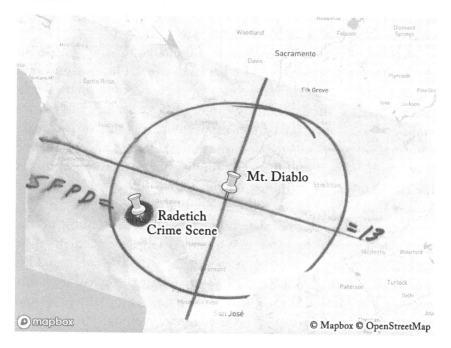

Figure 3.4: The annotated Zodiac symbol from the *Mikado* Letter, centered on Mt. Diablo and rotated 17° per the killer's methodology. The overemphasized "0" is drawn to indicate the Richard Radetich crime scene.

3.9.1 Speculative Evolution

With the botched Kathleen Johns outing receding into the past, the killer started to consider the summer solstice. A logical choice would be to return to the rope quadrant and finish the job he started on March 22. However, apart from the single *Examiner* article, the drama surrounding the Johns incident had not made much of an impact on the Bay Area. This, combined with the fact that it had been several months since his last murder—that of Paul Stine—were conspiring to make the killer less relevant than he desired. Writing to the media provided the man with some degree of satisfaction, but his crimes—the fundamental thing that generated the fear he so perversely thrived upon—had stagnated. Upon reflection, the solution to the problem was obvious: he needed to commit his next murder in San Francisco.

And so, as the rest of the Bay Area prepared for another Northern California summer, the killer began to convert his thoughts into actions. He decided to kill somebody, possibly a couple, on the weekend of June 21—the date of the summer solstice. Per his standard operating procedure, the man made one or more trial runs on the weekends preceding the solstice. Clearly, the murder of Officer Radetich was a crime of opportunity, so it's impossible to know the details of the killer's original intentions. Whatever they may have been, we can be sure that he engaged in some amount of preparation.

He probably started searching for potential victims in the predawn hours of the same day he killed Officer Radetich. If he had failed to find an acceptable victim, he would've continued his search on Saturday. Likewise, if Saturday failed to yield a victim, he would've continued the effort on Sunday. The goal was to find an acceptable victim (or victims) by Sunday evening. Furthermore, the killer preferred to strike while it was dark to facilitate his escape since San Francisco is an inherently challenging environment given its population, traffic, and police presence. Early morning or late evening did not matter; darkness was the main requirement. The other constraint he concerned himself with was crime-scene accommodation. For example, he needed to make sure that the streets were not crowded and that there was a reasonable avenue for escape. These latter requirements automatically ruled out some areas of San Francisco during the night. Otherwise, all locations in the general vicinity of the position 8 radial line were on the table.

The killer likely left his home in the wee hours of Friday, June 19 with the intention of targeting his standard victim profile (in his preferred order): (a) a couple, (b) a lone woman, or (c) other victim(s). However, he knew that finding a couple at this time of day would be challenging. He'd also have to deal with the complexity of killing two people and still making his escape. As we know happened with Officer Radetich, the killer shot quickly and left immediately because he understood the precariousness of his circumstances. If he sought two victims, not only would he be required to shoot twice as much, but the likelihood of something going wrong would increase disproportionately, thereby increasing the probability of the killer being seen or apprehended. Certainly, if he came across a couple under ideal circumstances, he would act. But, at the same time, he likely accepted that he would have to settle for option (b) or (c).

Just two months prior, in his "My Name Is" Letter, the Zodiac did express a perverse appreciation for the idea of "killing a cop," but I doubt he set out on the morning of June 19 specifically planning to take the life of a police officer. Undoubtedly, if he had encountered a patrol car with two officers instead of one, he would have hesitated to take them on. However, when he came across the solitary Officer Radetich in an isolated and quiet area, the opportunity to gun down a member of the SFPD was likely too good to pass up. The Zodiac felt he had been irrevocably wronged by the SFPD, particularly Martin Lee, and this scenario provided him a chance to exact revenge. Sadly for Officer Radetich, he was yet another person who was in the wrong place, at the wrong time, under the wrong circumstances.

More than likely, the Zodiac sped away from the Radetich crime scene and returned to his residence where he readied himself to show up at work a short while later. In the days that followed, the killer crafted his Button Letter. Intent on remaining ambiguous the man played it coy by making a thinly veiled reference to the young officer's murder, describing him only as "a man sitting in a car." Likely, the killer was surprised, perversely amused, and also disappointed that the sole focus of the SFPD's investigation was on Joe Allen Johnson, a man who had nothing to do with the crime. Regardless, the Zodiac had the excitement of his Phillips 66 map project and its associated cipher to keep him distracted from the Johnson situation.

3.10   Donna Lass | September 6, 1970

It's a sad and ironic twist of fate that Donna Lass would fall victim to the Zodiac after having moved from the killer's primary area of operation to South Lake Tahoe, some 200 miles away. While no one in San Francisco was safe from the Zodiac, Donna was a more likely victim, given that she was a lone woman who worked at Letterman General Hospital — an army hospital in the Presidio — and, hence, in close proximity to where Paul Stine was killed. But once Donna moved away, the chances of her falling prey to the Zodiac seemed nonexistent. Ultimately, this is just one of the many details of the case that inexplicably defies explanation.

The facts surrounding Donna's disappearance are puzzling: police found her vehicle at her apartment, there were no signs of a struggle, an anonymous male phoned her landlord and employer with a fabricated story about a family emergency, and, of course, her body was never found. Of all the extended crimes of the Zodiac, this one is the most mysterious and yields the fewest satisfying answers.

As shown in Figure 3.5, position 1 of the rotated compass rose intersects the northwest corner of Lake Tahoe. As was the case with Lake Berryessa, the killer likely considered the entire lake fair game given that the position 1 radial line passes through the body of water. Or, again, he may have been less concerned with perfect alignment by this point in his criminal evolution — the disappearance and presumptive murder of Donna Lass was the last crime reasonably attributed to the Zodiac. Either way, the dual cities of South Lake Tahoe, California and Stateline, Nevada — which straddle the California-Nevada border — were, and remain, a popular destination for Bay Area residents who are attracted to the region's alpine beauty, world-class skiing, and legal gambling in Nevada's casinos. These attributes made the South Lake Tahoe area a logical hunting ground for a position 1 victim.

Moreover, position 1 was in the knife quadrant. Again, as was the case in Lake Berryessa, the challenges posed by perpetrating a murder with a knife would have required that the killer engage in some

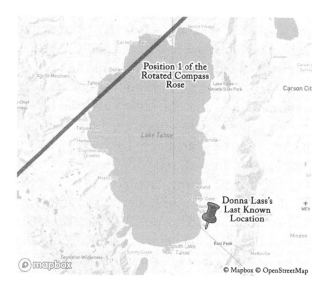

Figure 3.5: The intersection of the position 1 radial line and Lake Tahoe.

sort of premeditated situational control, which is consistent with the state of the evidence: there were no signs of a struggle and nothing seemed out of the ordinary. In fact, the anonymous phone calls made to Donna's landlord and employer were likely part of the killer's premeditated situational control, albeit taken to a new level. These circumstances also suggest that the killer somehow convinced Donna to provide the phone numbers.

The precise ruse that the killer used to gain control over Donna is unknowable. All we can say is that it was an effective bit of manipulation, and it left little in the way of usable evidence. Just as it would have been impossible to know exactly how the killer managed to ensnare Kathleen Johns had she not escaped and lived to tell her story, in the case of Donna, we simply do not know what happened. What we do know, however, is that Donna chose a career as a nurse, so caring for other people was literally her life's work. In all likelihood, if Donna believed that somebody was truly in need, she would not have hesitated to help. Unfortunately, this admirable disposition would have played right into the hands of the Bay Area killer.

The most troubling aspect of Donna Lass's presumptive murder is the fact that her remains have never been found. As somebody who thrived on the publicity surrounding his crimes and correspondence, the killer must have intended for somebody to discover the body. The most probable scenario is that the killer kidnapped Donna — as he had done with Kathleen Johns — murdered her, and then dumped her body in a semi-secluded area near Lake Tahoe. It is possible he selected a location that aligned well with the position 1 radial line of the rotated compass rose. If true, Donna's remains would be some-where in the northwest region of Lake Tahoe rather than the area in which she was abducted. This possibility makes sense given the evidence provided by the anonymous Christmas Card sent from the Bay Area to Donna's sister Mary Pilker in 1974, which referenced "St. Donna & Guardian of the Pines."

What the killer likely did not count on is that Lake Tahoe's se-cludedness, weather, and wildlife all conspired to deprive the world of the discovery of Donna's remains. Fate ensured that whatever no-toriety the man fantasized about savoring in the wake of somebody stumbling across Donna's lifeless body continued to be just that, a fantasy. Of course, by this point, the killer had a fair amount of prac-tice dealing with events not working out according to plan. Although there were clearly other dynamics at work that would soon lead the killer to suspend his actions, he nevertheless sent the Peek Through the Pines Card to commemorate the spring equinox and point inves-tigators in the direction of Donna's disappearance.

3.10.1   Speculative Evolution

Dealing with the disappointment of the SFPD's misguided focus on Joe Allen Johnson for the death of Officer Radetich and Paul Avery's surprisingly simplistic attempt at interpreting the meaning of the Phillips 66 map sent along with the Button Letter (see Section 5.2.5 of *The Zodiac Revisited, Volume 2*), the Zodiac turned his attention to the autumnal equinox. The killer decided to focus on the position 1 radial line of the rotated compass rose, likely because it was one of the few remaining, unused positions.

As the killer analyzed the regions associated with position 1, he noticed how it intersected Lake Tahoe. The thought of striking in or around Lake Tahoe was appealing for a couple of reasons. First, as mentioned previously, the region was a popular destination for Bay Area residents and, therefore, one could think it of as having a San Francisco connection. Second, Lake Tahoe is reasonably far away from the Bay Area and is literally on the Nevada border. By targeting someone at this distance from the Bay Area, the killer was expanding his particular form of domestic terrorism and, in so doing, extending his reach to include all of California.

Of course, the logistics of striking in Lake Tahoe were more complicated than those of his previous crimes. Accordingly, the killer took advantage of the three-day Labor Day weekend by driving from the Bay Area to Lake Tahoe on the morning of Saturday, September 5. Initially, the plan was probably just to become familiar with the area in preparation for returning two or three weeks later — in 1970, the autumnal equinox landed in the middle of the week, on Wednesday, September 23. The killer had settled on abducting a young woman, murdering her with a knife, and dumping the body in a semi-secluded area. He'd already crafted most, if not all, of the ruse he'd use to ensnare his victim, but the remaining details were still up in the air.

After driving several hours and arriving in Lake Tahoe, the killer started to have second thoughts about returning at a later date. Given the logistics, a normal weekend would likely yield only one evening during which he could reasonably find a victim. And if things didn't work out on that evening, he'd have to drive back a third time for another attempt. He could conceivably take a day off work, but doing that might draw attention to himself. Even being away for Labor Day and one or two subsequent weekends might be suspicious, especially if news of the murder was covered in the Bay Area media. There's no doubt the killer was paranoid, but it was this paranoia that allowed him to avoid apprehension.

Perhaps during this time, the man reflected on recent history. He had commemorated the winter solstice simply by writing the Belli

Letter, largely because he had moved his original plans for the event (the Stine murder) to October 1969. The spring equinox had been a disaster, all because he had the unfortunate luck of abducting a woman who, unbeknownst to him, had a baby in the car. The killer had been more successful with the murder of Officer Radetich during the summer solstice, but ironically, it mattered little since police were ignoring the possibility that he was responsible. To make matters worse, nobody seemed to understand the game that the killer was playing. Even *Chronicle* reporter Paul Avery, one of the people who was most knowledgeable about the case, had failed miserably at interpreting the Phillips 66 map. All in all, very few things had worked out as well as the killer had hoped.

Taking all of these factors into consideration, the Zodiac decided that the crime itself was more important than its precise alignment with the autumnal equinox. As such, the killer resolved that if he could find a victim during the Labor Day weekend trip, he'd follow through with his plan. The timing was a bit early, but it was acceptable. Unfortunately for Donna Lass, the killer did manage to find his victim.

In the days and weeks after Labor Day, the killer waited with a strange sense of eager patience for the world to take notice of his grisly misdeed. Much to his dismay, nothing happened. Around the time of the autumnal equinox, the *Chronicle* covered the strange disappearance of Donna Lass from her residence near South Lake Tahoe.[30] The killer was certainly pleased that the Bay Area paper covered the mystery so near to the equinox, even if that had not been his original intention. In just a few months, winter once again visited upon the Sierra Nevadas, and with its arrival the likelihood of someone finding Donna disappeared for another season. As spring turned to summer, decomposition and wildlife activity likely joined forces to ensure that Donna's remains would be nearly impossible to find. Once again, the killer's immediate hope to bask in the attention of his criminal infamy went unrealized.

As hinted at a few years later in the Red Phantom Letter, the man behind the Zodiac persona may have been under some form of psychiatric care by this point (see Section 2.19). The rigors of treatment, the passing of time, and the influence of medication all may have worked together to change the mental state of the killer. What was once an unwavering commitment to his deadly deeds had diminished to the point of occasional ambivalence. In the weeks and months that follow the autumnal equinox, his psychological condition evolved to the point where he began to consider stepping away from the deadly game he'd been playing. Nonetheless, in this time frame, the killer maintained a deep desire to be understood, or more precisely, figured out, which moved him to send Paul Avery the third-most meaningful clue in the collection of Zodiac correspondence, the Halloween Card.*

Interestingly, the lack of a significant development near the winter solstice is, itself, a significant development. For the first time in a year and a half, the killer refrained from acting in conjunction with a solstice or equinox — no criminal action, no letter, nothing. This lack of activity was particularly important given that the killer considered the winter solstice special. As discussed in Section 3.2.3.1 of *The Zodiac Revisited, Volume 2*, the symbolism associated with the yearly happening had likely motivated the man to wait until December 1968 to commit his first murders in the Bay Area. In a very real sense, the winter solstice represented the birth of the Zodiac persona. The killer neglecting this date of self-assigned significance illustrates the extent of the transformation that the man's psyche was undergoing.

However, the killer's psychological progress was unpredictable and inconsistent, which is why, after choosing not to act during the winter solstice, the man regressed and sent the pasted-up Peek Through the Pines Card and the *Los Angeles Times* Letter to correspond with the vernal equinox. But these deeds were merely the vestiges of his former self, the last authentic actions of the Zodiac before his nearly three-year hiatus.

---

*The first two are the annotated Phillips 66 map and the *X*'ed Zodiac symbol.

3.11 Conclusion

In seven years' time, an unknown psychopath committed ten violent crimes, and in the process took the lives of twelve young men and women. These men and women had the potential for living long and productive lives, full of happiness and achievement. The killer's diabolical deeds caused death, destruction, suffering, and grief. In the aftermath of these senseless tragedies, the victims' families and friends were continually haunted by what might have been. But by the end of 1970, the mental anomaly that had compelled the killer to murder fellow human beings had run its course, or, more precisely, progressed to a point where it no longer manifested into the malignancy of murder. Unfortunately, planning, discipline, some undeniable skill, and a good bit of luck allowed the killer to emerge from this period of his life unapprehended by law enforcement. Although he probably didn't appreciate it at the time, when the man returned to the Bay Area following the murder of Donna Lass, he would never again act on an intention to kill.

Notes

1. Ressler, Robert K. and Shachtman, Tom, *Whoever Fights Monsters: My Twenty Years Hunting Serial Killers for the FBI*, New York: St. Martin's Press, 1992, p. 116.

2. "Beach Sniper Slayer Still Eludes Detection," *The San Diego Union*, April 6, 1964, A–9.

3. Paul Avery, "New Evidence in Zodiac Killings," *San Francisco Chronicle*, November 16, 1970, 1.

4. Paul Avery, "Zodiac Link Is Definite," *San Francisco Chronicle*, November 17, 1970, 2.

5. John Montgomery, "'Your Daughter May Be Next'," *Inside Detective*, January 1969, 59.

6. "Knife Killer's Victim Buried in Crestlawn," *The Press*, November 4, 1966, B2.

7. "Sniper Slaying Probers Seek Ex-Resident," *The San Diego Union*, February 23, 1964, A–15.

8. "Coed Stabbed to Death on Riverside College Campus," *Los Angeles Times*, November 1, 1966, 3.

9. "Police File 352-481 Gets Thicker; Cheri Bates Murder Case Month Old," *The Press*, November 30, 1966, B1.

10. "Typed Confession Letter Receives Close Attention of Police Experts," *The Press*, November 30, 1966, B1.

11. George McEvoy, "Friends Quizzed in Slaying of Teen Pair Near Vallejo," *San Francisco Sunday Examiner & Chronicle*, December 22, 1968, A10.

12. "Teen Pair 'Executed' Near Vallejo," *San Francisco Examiner*, December 21, 1968, 1.

13. "Hunt Maniac in Murders of Teenagers," *Vallejo Times-Herald*, December 23, 1968, 1, 8.

14. Robert Graysmith, *Zodiac*, New York: St. Martin's Press, 1986.

15. Kelleher, Michael D. and Van Nuys, David, *"This Is the Zodiac Speaking": Into the Mind of a Serial Killer*, Westport, Connecticut: Praeger, 2002.

16. Jim Lovett, "Continuation Report: Case No. C62677," March 23, 1970.

17. "Rode with Zodiac, Woman Claims," *San Francisco Examiner*, March 23, 1970, 4.

18. Johns, Kathleen, interview by Johnny Smith and Howard Davis, "H. J. N. Terprises, Inc.," January 1, 1998, audio recording.

19. Robert Graysmith, *Zodiac*, New York: Berkley Books, 1987.

20. "Mystery Gunman Kills S.F. Officer," *San Francisco Chronicle*, June 20, 1970, 1.

21. Frank O'Mea, "Two Policemen Per Car," *San Francisco Chronicle*, June 21, 1970, 1.

22. George Murphy, "A Man's Full Circle," *San Francisco Chronicle*, June 23, 1970, 1.

23. Carolyn Anspacher, "A Day for Slain Officer," *San Francisco Chronicle*, January 3, 1970, 4.

24. Paul Avery, "Slain Policeman Lies in State," *San Francisco Chronicle*, June 22, 1970, 3.

25. "Suspect in Shooting of Patrolman," *San Francisco Chronicle*, June 23, 1970, 1.

26. George Murphy, "Bay Manhunt for Suspected Killer," *San Francisco Chronicle*, June 24, 1970, 1.

27. "Nelder Heads Wide Search for Suspect," *San Francisco Examiner*, June 23, 1970, 1.

28. "Arraignment in Slaying of Police Officer," *San Francisco Chronicle*, December 22, 1970, 4.

29. Ernest Lenn, "Police Murder Count Stopped," *San Francisco Chronicle*, January 10, 1971, 3.

30. "Nurse Vanishes — A Tahoe Mystery," *San Francisco Chronicle*, September 26, 1970, 3.

CHAPTER

4

Final Thoughts

...for all meanings, we know, depend on the key of interpretation.

George Eliot, *Daniel Deronda*, 1876

In the previous chapters, we have made numerous observations regarding all aspects of the Zodiac case. We've reviewed the facts of the case, analyzed the important threads woven throughout the fabric of the evidence, reconsidered and reinterpreted the killer's letters and his crimes based on this newfound understanding, and translated the resulting knowledge into a possible evolution. To reach this point in our shared journey, we've traveled far and, along the way, developed much insight into the killer and his crimes.

In this final segment of our analytical travels, I'll step back and draw some conclusions about the man who was the Zodiac. Based on the collective consideration and reconsideration of the evidence, what can we say about him? What identifiable characteristics stand out? What points of speculation are reasonably supported? By addressing these questions, we'll arrive at a clearer picture of this as-of-yet unidentified murderer who terrorized so many, so well.

Residence

The evidence suggests that the killer invested significant time and effort into the formulation and execution of the three Southern California crimes, which resulted in the deaths of five victims. As discussed in Section 3.1, if we triangulate the crime scenes, the resulting shape represents the killer's theater of operation. Likely, the man lived within the confines of this triangle between June 1963 and April 1967. To perpetrate his crimes, he planned and traveled significant, but not prohibitive, distances to minimize the likelihood of his identification and capture. Of particular note, Los Angeles exists within this triangle at some considerable distance to all three crime scenes. Hence, there's a reasonably good chance that the killer resided somewhere inside the Greater Los Angeles area.

Between April 1967 and December 1968, the man likely moved from Southern California to the San Francisco Bay Area. Despite what many others believe, he almost certainly did not live in or near Vallejo. Also, because he was unable to name Cherry Street, it seems that he was unfamiliar with the Presidio Heights neighborhood, so it's unlikely that he lived in that particular section of San Francisco. However, it's possible that he lived anywhere else in the Bay Area.

Never Fingerprinted

As evidenced by the number and quality of fingerprints that law enforcement obtained from the letters and crime-scene evidence, the man was not concerned with being identified through this well-known forensic means. This fact suggests that the man had supreme confidence that his fingerprints could not be used to identify him, which can only be true if he *knew* that he had never been fingerprinted. As discussed earlier in Section 2.6, this scenario is consistent with the interpretation of the killer creating "busy work" for law enforcement. Hence, the man likely had avoided any experience that would have involved fingerprinting, for example being arrested or serving in the military.

Mentally Disciplined

The Zodiac managed to exist for many years in an environment where hundreds, if not thousands, of people had invested considerable time and effort into identifying him. Yet, more likely than not, he never acted in a way that raised the suspicions of anybody whom he encountered. Furthermore, the man was clearly frustrated in terms of not being understood. Be it Paul Avery's simplistic and clearly incorrect interpretation of the Phillips 66 map, the inability of people to decipher any of the three unsolved cryptograms (the killer almost certainly expected people to solve at least one, if not two or all three), or the death-threat interpretation of the Halloween Card, the man had expectations of law enforcement, the press, and the public that simply did not pan out. Through all of this frustration, however, only once did he provide an explicit clue regarding what he meant, in the form of the infamous radian postscript. And when that didn't produce the desired result, he moved on. Less disciplined people, such as Dennis Rader (BTK) after his reemergence in 2004, would have acted until they had the satisfaction of their secret communication being revealed, until the self-perceived genius behind their madness was known to the world. The Zodiac just let it go. Relatedly, Rader is behind bars; the Zodiac remains at large.

The bad news is that if the killer ever decided to minimize the likelihood of being identified — and he may have reached such a conclusion — he would have had no qualms about destroying any evidence that could link him to his crimes. If this was the case, we're unlikely to have a relative find the remains of Paul Stine's shirt, Johnny Ray Swindle's driver's license, or any other possession that could definitively identify him as the Zodiac. Of particular note, when he reemerged in 1974 to send his final letters, he could have verified his identity by including another swatch of Stine's bloodstained shirt. Instead, he chose to rely on the uniqueness of his handwriting, for example, consciously using an excessive number of circles instead of dots. The implication, of course, is that he may have already disposed of the remainder of Stine's shirt. Albeit, in this case, the killer was clearly having psychological difficulty donning his persona one last time, so he may have simply been unwilling to use the bloodstained shirt.

This is not to say that events necessarily played out this way. It's possible that the killer didn't destroy any evidence and just kept it in his possession. The observation is simply that if he did reach such a conclusion, he would have had the mental discipline to act upon it.

Knowledge of Celestial Navigation

Whether or not you agree with the specific methodologies I've proposed in *The Zodiac Revisited, Volume 2*, it's difficult to argue against the observations that (a) the annotated Zodiac symbol from the Phillips 66 map is derived from the concept of the compass rose, (b) the compass rose is a fundamental component of nautical navigation, and (c) the zodiac (in a nonastrological sense) is an important concept of celestial navigation. It's an almost certainty that the killer had some degree of knowledge about nautical and celestial navigation. The exact nature of how the man came to have this knowledge, of course, remains unclear. He may have had a paramilitary interest in the navy or knowledge of nautical navigation through some tangential relationship. All we can really say is that there would have been some basis for the knowledge, and it likely did not come from his own personal military service.

If the man had any substantive relationships with people in his life, such as coworkers, friends, or family, he may well have volunteered information about nautical navigation or the nonastrological meaning of the zodiac, mostly in the form of statements or questions designed to demonstrate his depth of knowledge. Examples of what this might have looked like include:

- Did you know that magnetic north changes with time?
- Did you know that magnetic north can be significantly different from true north?

- People who like astrology don't even understand what the zodiac actually is.

- Did you know there's a scientific basis for the zodiac?

- The winter solstice is the longest night of the year.

- After the winter solstice, the days get longer and longer, up until the summer solstice.

Employment

The San Diego and Riverside attacks were committed on a Wednesday and Sunday evening, respectively. Robert Domingos and Linda Edwards, however, were murdered on a Tuesday, likely in the afternoon. The killer almost certainly made a special trip to Riverside to mail The Confession from one of the city's public mailboxes. The letters were postmarked on a Tuesday, further suggesting that Tuesday was a day of the week when the man was able to pursue his murderous exploits.

By the time the killer moved north and assumed the persona of the Zodiac, he was restricting most of his activity to weekends. These facts suggest that in the Bay Area, the killer was holding down some type of conventional nine-to-five job that prevented him from acting at other times. In Southern California, the situation is less clear. He may have had a job with less conventional hours that afforded him the opportunity to strike on a Tuesday afternoon. That's the most probable explanation. Or he may have been a student during this time frame, perhaps pursuing an undergraduate degree or even a graduate degree. Finally, there's always the chance that he was unemployed. In the final analysis, we can't really say much about his employment during the time of the Southern California murders.

If we were able to identify the Zodiac and talk to people who worked with him during his reign of terror in the Bay Area, I suspect most of them would register little more than surprise and shock, apart from the unsurprising "he was quiet and kept to himself." It's possible some might have noted peculiar behaviors that, in retrospect, would begin to make sense. But it's unlikely that anyone was actively suspicious of him. This is an area in which his mental discipline would have played an active role. He would have done nothing to draw the unwanted attention of anyone at work. He would have played the part of an exceptionally good rule follower, always being on time and following processes to a tee. He probably would not have aspired to substantive career advancement. But he would have executed his existing duties in a way that did not attract attention to himself—the primary focus would have been on negative attention, although he probably also acted to limit positive attention.

Social Shallowness

The killer had the ability to appear normal for short periods of time when the situation called for it. He knew what normal was; he knew what it looked like; he knew how to mimic it. These are the skills that allowed the man to gain control of Cheri Jo Bates, Kathleen Johns, and to a lesser extent, Bryan Hartnell and Cecelia Shepard. Of course, he was not normal, and his pathology suggests he would not have been able to achieve normal, meaningful, long-term, adult relationships. People who interacted with him in a very limited social context, but possibly frequently, such as coworkers or neighbors, probably would have experienced the man's ability to mimic normal behavior. He likely would have worked hard to avoid substantive conversation, but the people who had short interactions with the man probably would have come away thinking he's a "good guy," albeit perhaps a bit odd.

Marital Status

The one prediction I would shy away from is concluding that the man never married. As we've seen in recent decades, there are multiple examples of prolific serial killers operating from domestic situations that include having a seemingly normal marriage and family. Such examples include Dennis Rader (BTK), Gary Ridgeway (the Green River Killer), and Joseph DeAngelo (the Golden State Killer). If the Zodiac was married, the marriage likely would have been atypical in one or more significant respects. But there's really little else we can reasonably speculate.

Military Wannabe

While the likelihood that the Zodiac served in the military is low, the evidence of *an interest* in the military is substantial. In fact, the case is replete with military references, such as ammunition that may have been purchased at a military PX, the shooting of a sailor and his wife, the use of cryptography, footprints left from military shoes, bomb diagrams inspired with improvised munitions, and a killer who was proficient in many types of weaponry. As with the more specific subject of nautical navigation, it's impossible to know exactly how the man acquired his knowledge of these various military subjects. Again, he may have benefited from a tangential relationship with someone, such as a family member or friend, who actually had military experience, or he may have developed the interest solely on his own and cultivated it through gun shows and other activities that would have provided access to military information.

In the two instances of military footwear in the evidence — the heel print from Riverside and the numerous wing-walker footprints at Lake Berryessa — investigators determined that members of the general public could have easily purchased the footgear in question. Hence, these important components of the evidence are perfectly consistent with a civilian who had a significant interest in various military subjects.

Newspaper Subscription

Much of the killer's behavior suggested that he was an avid newspaper reader. In and of itself, this observation is not surprising. At the time, newspapers were the predominant means of news dissemination, and many people read them on a daily basis.

As mentioned previously, at the time of the Southern California murders, it is likely that the killer lived in the Greater Los Angeles area. That being the case, there's a strong probability that he subscribed to the *Los Angeles Times*. This easily explains how the killer knew about the *Times*'s coverage of his earlier murders — assuming that the Zodiac was referring to the Southern California murders in the *Los Angeles Times* Letter. As with much of this speculation, we cannot be 100 percent sure, but there is a strong likelihood.

By the time the killer was operating in the Bay Area, there's an interesting dynamic buried in his actions. After the first two instances of letter writing, we know that the killer chose to write exclusively to the *Chronicle*, with the exception of the *Los Angeles Times* Letter. This was a logical choice because the *Chronicle* had the largest circulation of any Bay Area paper. Interestingly, however, when the killer reacted to news stories — other than the early ones from the *Vallejo Times-Herald* — it was often in reference to stories from the *Examiner*. The point-by-point refutation of Martin Lee in the Bus Bomb Letter came from the *Examiner*'s version of the story. The "My Name Is" cipher was also in response to an *Examiner* article. Both the Crackproof Card and the Peek Through the Pines Card included content clipped from the *Examiner*. Similarly, the reference to the North Bay in the Stine Letter likely came from the same newspaper. This prevalence of *Examiner* content suggests that the killer may have had a subscription to the *Examiner* and not the *Chronicle*.

There are a couple of reasons why the *Examiner* would have been a logical choice. First, the killer was undoubtedly interested in what both papers had to say. The killer's interest in the *Chronicle* is self-evident. However, during the time in question, the *Examiner* was also a preeminent newspaper, in many ways equal to the *Chronicle*. Moreover, there was a real possibility that one paper might provide substantively different coverage than the other, for example the *Examiner* covered the kidnapping of Kathleen Johns at the time of its occurrence, but the *Chronicle* did not. Having a subscription to both dailies might have been a red flag for a serial killer who liked to read about himself in the newspaper. Hence, he probably felt comfortable subscribing to only one of the two. Again, since he was writing almost exclusively to the *Chronicle*, he likely preferred not to subscribe to it since detectives might have tried to use the paper's list of subscribers as an investigative tool. He could easily purchase that paper on an as-needed basis. Therefore, subscribing to the *Examiner* makes sense.

If we had infinite resources and data at our disposal, it would be interesting to see what kind of commonality we could find by cross-referencing 1964 *Los Angeles Times* subscribers with subscribers to the *San Francisco Examiner* in 1970. Unfortunately, for a number of reasons, this is a practical impossibility.

Psychiatric Treatment

As described in Section 2.19, several aspects of the killer's reemergence in 1974 suggest that he had likely undergone some form of psychological or psychiatric treatment. This conclusion is drawn from the man's inability to fully don the Zodiac persona, the suicide symbolism associated with "killing off" said persona, the *Exorcist* symbolism, the thinly veiled remorse expressed in the *Badlands* rebuke, and the numerous aspects of the Red Phantom Letter diatribe, which was clearly written in response to Count Marco's whimsical musings on psychology.

The killer may have had treatment for years prior to 1974, and he may have continued treatment for years after. Invoking the familiar refrain to our analysis, we cannot say for certain. We can only conclude that he likely received treatment.

"My Name Is" ...

I won't presume to claim that my solution to the "My Name Is" cipher is correct beyond any reasonable doubt (see Section 5.2.4 of *The Zodiac Revisited, Volume 2*). The case, to its detriment, is already overrun with people who speak in such absolutes. However, I will say that the solution is a logical and viable one based on a solid understanding of the Zodiac's use of cipher and a thorough knowledge of the case. Furthermore, the solution's structure is consistent with my proposed solution to the killer's other cipher, the 32. In this sense, both solutions have a commonality that most other proposed solutions lack. Finally, because the "My Name Is" cipher clearly came in response to Dr. D. C. B. Marsh's challenge to the killer to construct a cipher containing his name, there is a reasonably strong probability that the ego-driven killer actually did just that, in one form or another. For these reasons, I would pay particular attention to any suspect whose name matched my proposed solution. To be sure, there is a possibility that the solution is incorrect and, even if it is correct, there were people living at the time with names that would fit the constraints of the cipher yet surely were not the Zodiac. Therefore, it's important to maintain objectivity and focus on the name in the solution as a single element and consider it in conjunction with other corroborating evidence. However, assuming those requirements are satisfied, the cipher constraints have the potential to prove valuable.

Education and Intelligence

What can we say about the educational accomplishments of our unknown subject? In terms of specifics, we can say little. However, there are several hints that provide us some indication of the type of man that we're dealing with.

First and foremost, there are the ciphers: four in total; two of substantial length. The remaining two are considerably shorter but, in many ways, no less thoughtful in their creation. As proposed earlier, it's certainly possible that a man with no knowledge of or inclination for cryptography could drudge his way through learning and crafting such a composition. But would he? The answer is, quite likely, no. Nor would the use of cipher appeal to such a person. The construction of these ciphers necessarily requires tedious, detail-oriented work. The creation of the content and the distribution of the symbols is inherently mathematical. Somebody who is enthusiastic about creating this type of puzzle would almost certainly be a mathematical, analytical, left-brained type of person.

The killer's two bus bomb diagrams and the electrical circuits required to make such incendiary devices reinforce this perception of the man. While the circuits are not sophisticated, they do indicate a basic knowledge of electronics. Again, this type of endeavor would appeal to an analytical mind. Moreover, the ability to take existing trigger mechanisms and incorporate them into an amalgam trigger mechanism as in the first bus bomb, and then evolve the flawed first circuit into the less deficient second circuit, illustrates a certain analytical creativity that is indicative of an underlying intelligence and possibly advanced academic accomplishment.

Of course, there's the infamous use of the word "radians," about which many people have speculated. If the possibility I suggested is true — that the killer used the word "radians" as a clue given its historical interpretation as a contraction of "radial angle," then I would suspect that the man had advanced training in mathematics. Otherwise, the interpretation is less clear. Some people argue that radians are very esoteric units. I disagree with this claim. Most of us learn about radians when taking trigonometry sometime in high school. The problem is, most people also forget about them soon after. Nevertheless, with the word being part of the killer's vernacular, this again suggests that he had significant exposure to mathematics.

Another indication of the killer's intelligence and probable education was his penchant for abstract thought, as evidenced by the symbolism seen in much of the case evidence. This symbolism came in at least two forms. The first was explicit. It was on display in the Zodiac's references to Ko-Ko, the Lord High Executioner who imposed a death sentence upon all who flirt. It was evidenced in the killer's reference to *The Exorcist* with its central theme of demonic possession. The second form was not so explicit, but it was equally, if not more, symbolic. Examples include instances of spatial information, such as the division of the Halloween Card into quadrants, the centering of the radian postscript on position 6, and the inclusion of the number 0 in a meaningful location when referring to Officer Radetich. In all these cases, the man was communicating information through abstract means rather than normal written language. This approach was highly symbolic.

Finally, there is the question of the killer's methodology as described in Chapter 3 of *The Zodiac Revisited, Volume 2.* It's complex and enigmatic. In some sense, it's an abstraction of murder itself in that the Zodiac didn't seem to care *whom* he killed, just *that* he killed, as long as his victims satisfied the constraints that he created for himself. In his mind, his victims were the wrong kind of people, and they were quite literally in the wrong place at the wrong time. This behavior was, once again, an instance of abstract thought. A twisted set of rules, self-constructed and self-imposed by a social deviant who derived tremendous pleasure from crossing society's most basic ethical boundary. These were not the machinations of a thoughtless man. Quite the contrary, they were the manifestations of an intelligent, albeit abnormal, mind.

As stated previously, I suggest the man who was the Zodiac likely possessed a considerable amount of intelligence. He was probably not a genius, as many people have suggested, nor was he likely to have been a brilliant academic like Ted Kaczynski. However, I expect that he could've completed a graduate degree, had the opportunity presented itself. Because he was severely lacking in social interactions, his intelligence would have been one of the few things that made him happy, so it is reasonable to assume that he may have pursued some amount of post-secondary education. However, given his evolving psychopathy, it is hard to say how far he got in pursuit of a degree. The most we can say is that he likely had a post-secondary education that fell somewhere between partial progress toward an undergraduate degree to completion of a graduate degree. Furthermore, the degree in question would have been something analytical and left-brained such as mathematics, the physical sciences, or engineering.

CHAPTER

5

Only Time Will Tell

It is the mark of an educated mind to rest satisfied with the degree of precision which the nature of the subject admits and not to seek exactness where only an approximation is possible.

Aristotle, 384–322 BCE

Daring to hope for closure in the case of the Zodiac has proven itself to be an exercise in self-delusion, frustration, or both. At the time of this book's publication, easily more than twenty people have convinced themselves that they know the killer's true identity and have publicly accused the target of their suspicion; and membership in that club is growing all the time. Few, however, have managed to convince much of the rest of the world, let alone law enforcement. Moreover, only one of the accused can actually *be* the killer. The rest are merely victims of another injustice.*

---

*The extent to which we should feel sympathy for these accused men based on this injustice varies. Some are impressive, contributing members of society who have no history of wrongdoing; others are murderers in their own right.

With this short chapter, yet another work on the Zodiac saga comes to an end. As I wrote at the start of this journey, it is my sincere hope that the contents of *The Zodiac Revisited* will make an incremental contribution to identifying the man who destroyed so much and terrorized so many. But only time will tell if that will ever happen.

Sadly, one thing is certain: most of the world has moved past the case of the Zodiac. Of the three victims who survived their ordeal with the killer, one has passed away* and the other two, understandably, have moved on with their lives in their own respective ways.† Many family members of the less fortunate victims have also passed on. All of the primary investigators are either retired or deceased. To put it simply, the people who had the most to gain from seeing the case solved are no longer with us to see it through.

Furthermore, the vacuum created by their absence has been filled with a diverse and often strange mix of people interested in the case. To be sure, there are serious, dedicated, and even professional individuals among their ranks. However, there are also many people who loudly advocate for positions of extreme speculation — positions that objective people who are knowledgeable about the case cannot take seriously.

Underlying this dynamic is the fact that most people just do not know what to make of the Zodiac. This statement describes the general public, but it also applies to the media and even many of the law enforcement organizations that have inherited the case. The combination of so many facts and so little certainty is simply a recipe for confusion.

In addition, members of law enforcement — though undeniably committed to their job — are simply tired of the constant drain that the public's fascination with the case has placed on their finite set of available resources.[2] In fact, in 2007 then SFPD Captain

---

*Kathleen Johns passed away in 2002.

†Bryan Hartnell became a successful attorney. Both he and Mike Mageau were featured in the documentaries released with the director's cut of the 2007 movie *Zodiac*.[1]

John Hennessey once summed up his thoughts on the matter by explaining: "I hate that case. It just sucks the oxygen out of everything around it."[3] Admittedly, solving the crime at this point effectively does little in terms of the administration of justice; the time for that has long since come and gone. As uncomfortable as it is to admit, the Zodiac got away with his crimes. All a solution would really do now is satisfy a sense of historical curiosity. Moreover, practicality requires that law enforcement prioritize current cases over a decades-old cold case that has remained unsolved despite a massive expenditure of effort. Therefore, the future priority of the Zodiac case will, almost certainly, never again be high.

Any honest evaluation of the situation suggests that we are further away from a solution now than we were in the early to mid-1970s, advancements in DNA technology notwithstanding. Yet, as dire as the situation seems, we must maintain hope. At any given moment, we are never more than a single important discovery away from the ever-elusive answer. Perhaps that discovery will come in the form of a legitimate decipherment of one of the killer's cryptograms, put forth tomorrow. Perhaps it will involve some future advancement in DNA analysis applied to a descendant of the killer a hundred years from now. Or, perhaps it will be a development of a less predictable nature at some point in between.

Thus far, the future has been largely unkind to those of us interested in the Zodiac case. The passage of time has done little more than germinate seeds of doubt and, in the process, render topics thought to be well understood considerably less so. But in the end, any hope we have for solving the case lies in the future. Five decades into this mystery, the actions taken to conceal the killer's identity — whether the intentional actions of the killer himself or the inadvertent actions of those indirectly involved — are now in the past. The mystery, forged in the crucible of the late 1960s and early 1970s and then tempered through the passage of the ensuing decades, will get no more difficult. It is as perplexing as it will ever be. It's up to us to keep the case alive and seriously consider the plethora of open questions. In so doing, we'll create a future that holds the potential for real progress; a future that will provide the answers to questions that, today, make no sense; a future that holds the promise of yielding the ever-elusive answer. I maintain a sense of optimism. I hope you'll join me. Together we can look forward to the day when somebody convinces the truly objective among us that the Zodiac was a man by the name of...

Notes

1. David Fincher, director, *Zodiac*, Paramount Pictures, 2007.

2. John Mikulenka, director, *Hunting the Zodiac*, Independent, 2007.

3. Ken Garcia, *SFPD Not Thrilled About Spotlight on Zodiac*, February 22, 2007, Accessed November 25, 2020, *http://zodiacrevisited.com/book/sfe-2007-02-22*.

A Request to the Reader

If you are reading these words, you have quite likely just finished *The Zodiac Revisited, Volume 3.* For this, I wish to express my appreciation. This increasingly busy world inundates each of us with a never-ending supply of subjects that vie for our attention. That you chose to spend some of your valuable time reading the book that I labored over for a considerable part of my life means a great deal to me. *I thank you.*

Before letting you move on, please allow me to ask a favor. As an independent author, the primary hope I have for achieving some modest degree of success lies in convincing readers of *The Zodiac Revisited* to review the work. As someone who has just read the last word of the last page, you are an ideal candidate.

Therefore, I would like to ask that you **please take a few minutes to document your thoughts about *The Zodiac Revisited* in the form of a review.** Doing so will be helpful not only to me, but also to the thousands of people each year who develop a fascination with history's most enigmatic serial killer.

This link will forward you to the appropriate location:

http://zodiacrevisited.com/review-vol3

Thank you for your time and consideration.

— Michael F. Cole

Be sure to get the rest of the story with
The Zodiac Revisited Volumes 1 and 2...

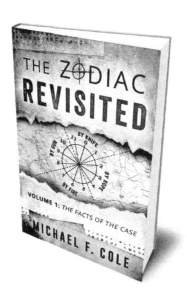 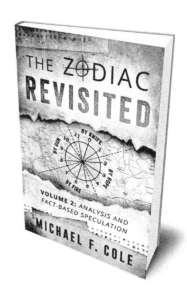

http://zodiacrevisited.com/vol1

http://zodiacrevisited.com/vol2

Index